SOMETHING RICH AND STRANGE

SELECTED ESSAYS ON SAM SELVON

EDITED AND INTRODUCED BY MARTIN ZEHNDER

PEEPAL TREE

First published in Great Britain in 2003
Peepal Tree Press Ltd
17 King's Avenue
Leeds LS6 1QS
England

ISBN 1 900715 73 2

Peepal Tree Press acknowledges financial support from Arts Council
England, Yorkshire.

Full fathom five thy father lies;
Of his bones are coral made;
Those are pearls that were his eyes;
Nothing of him that doth fade
But doth suffer a sea-change
Into something rich and strange.

William Shakespeare, *The Tempest*

For he knew now how to go about searching for knowledge. And the power – why, the power was all around him, he could feel it throbbing in the earth, humming in the air, riding the night wind, stealing through the swamp. The power was free, all you had to do was breathe it in, deep and full, until your chest felt like bursting.

Sam Selvon, *A Brighter Sun*

CONTENTS

ACKNOWLEDGEMENTS

This book on Samuel Selvon is the product of a one-year MA course at the University of Warwick and was compiled while writing my dissertation on Sam Selvon in the summer of 2000. I am therefore heavily indebted to my professors and supervisors at Warwick: to Professor David Dabydeen for making this publication possible and for being a most innovative and entertaining teacher, whose classes regularly lasted until the morning hours; to Professor Neil Lazarus for his unquenched personal and scholarly commitment all year long. I am also grateful to have been taught by the exceptional Professor Benita Parry, whose knowledge and style has left a lasting impression. I want to thank my friends, who made my year at Warwick a most memorable experience. My dearest thanks go out to Laura Vroomen. Her immaculate taste in music, wisdom and criticism have been wonderful companions – and still are to the present day. I would like to express my gratitude to Ewoud Pronk, Satoko Fujiwara, Jane Poyner, Maria Sfakianaki, Juliette Taylor, Nick Wong, and, of course, Tiro Sebina.

I owe an incalculable debt to three professors at the University of Zurich, Switzerland: Peter Hughes, Therese Steffen, and Kurt Spillmann have either through academic and/or personal support made my stay at Warwick possible. I am also grateful to the British Council for offering me a generous scholarship. Finally, I want to use this opportunity to express my respect and love for the following people who have helped me out in one way or another: Roman Koller, Viktor Bänziger, Christoph Brunner, Oreste Donadio, Claudia Laubscher, Roland Treyer, Alexandra Weiss – and, of course, my parents and my sister Karin. I dedicate this book to my late friend Asres Tesfaye, whose death six years ago left too many discussions unfinished.

Martin Zehnder
University of Warwick/Zurich, 1 May 2003

The editor would like to thank the following for permission to reproduce copyrighted material:

'Sam Selvon's Tiger: In Search of Self-Awareness' is reprinted from *Reworlding: The Literature of the Indian Diaspora* edited by Emmanuel S. Nelson (1993) with the kind permission of Greenwood Publishing Group, Inc., Westport, CT.

'The Male Mind and the Female Heart: Selvon's Ways to Knowledge in the "Tiger Books"' (*Caribana*, 5, 1996, pp.117-125) and '"Oldtalk": Two Interviews with Sam Selvon' (*Caribana*, 1, 1990, pp.71-84) are reprinted with the kind permission of *Caribana*.

'"The World Turn Upside Down": Carnival Patterns in *The Lonely Londoners*' (*The Toronto South Asian Review*, 5, Summer 1986, pp.191-204) is reprinted with the kind permission of John Thieme and *The Toronto South Asian Review*.

'The Philosophy of Neutrality: The Treatment of Political Militancy in Samuel Selvon's *Moses Ascending* and *Moses Migrating*' is reprinted from *Literature and Commitment: A Commonwealth Perspective* edited by Govind Narain Sharma (1988) with the kind permission of Victor J. Ramraj and *The Toronto South Asian Review*.

'Samuel Selvon's Linguistic Extravaganza: *Moses Ascending*' is reprinted from *Critical Issues in West Indian Literature* edited by Erika Sollish Smilowitz and Roberta Quarles Knowles (1984) with the kind permission of Caribbean Books.

'Comedy as Evasion in the Later Novels of Sam Selvon' is printed with the kind permission of Kenneth Ramchand. An earlier version of the essay appeared in *The Comic Vision in West Indian Literature* edited by Roydon Salick (1988).

'The Odyssey of Sam Selvon's Moses' is reprinted from *Nationalism vs. Internationalism: (Inter)National Dimensions of Literatures in English* edited by Wolfgang Zach and Ken L. Goodwin (1996) with the kind permission of Stauffenburg Verlag.

The primary sources of the bibliography are reprinted from *Foreday Morning: Selected Prose 1946-1986* edited by Kenneth Ramchand and Susheila Nasta (1989) with the kind permission of Susheila Nasta.

for Asres Tesfaye (d. 1997),
with gratitude

INTRODUCTION

MARTIN ZEHNDER

Though Sam Selvon published ten novels and a collection of short stories, and contributed a great number of short stories, poems and essays to newspapers and magazines, the critical assessment of his oeuvre has centred around the 'Tiger and Moses books'. His first novel, *A Brighter Sun*, as well as *The Lonely Londoners* and *Moses Ascending*, and to a lesser extent *Turn Again Tiger* and *Moses Migrating*, have elicited the most academic interest. In this sense, the present collection of essays reflects proportionally the focus of previous scholarly work, but it also opens up some significant new areas of attention.

The collection starts with Harold Barratt's essay 'Sam Selvon's Tiger: In Search of Self-Awareness', which deals with *A Brighter Sun* and its sequel, *Turn Again Tiger*. Barratt's contribution is helpful in various regards. Firstly, it places *A Brighter Sun* in the context of the West Indian literary renaissance of the 1950s and 1960s. Secondly, it shows that Selvon was an early explorer of what have become compelling issues in West Indian literature: identity, self-awareness and wholeness in colonial and ethnically plural societies that still bear the psychic scars of slavery and the equally dehumanising system of indentured labour. And thirdly, apart from Kenneth Ramchand[1] and Roydon Salick,[2] Barratt is one of the few critics who, despite rightly seeing Tiger's journey as one towards creolisation, does not neglect the Indo-Caribbean elements in the novel and Selvon's implicit argument that space has to be found for these within an expanded concept of creolisation.

As Clem Seecharan has importantly established:

> To the East Indian the earth is the bountiful mother ever ready to yield her
> rich stores of treasures to those who approach her in the right spirit... as
> soon as his term of indenture has expired and he once breathes the air of
> freedom, he turns with a glad heart to mother earth to wrest some of the
> treasures from her beneficent keeping.[3]

Barratt's argument, for recognising Tiger's continuing Indianness, goes
along the same lines, stressing the intimate bond between Tiger and the
land, which gives him a sense of oneness and solace:

> Sometimes, in the morning when he got up early and dew was still heavy
> on the grass, he used to watch at what he could see of the world – the sky,
> light blue with promises of a sunlit day, the low hills that break away from
> the Northern Range and run hunchbacked for some miles, and the trees
> on the hills, dark green before the sun rose and made them lighter. With
> all this... he felt a certain satisfaction, as if he were living in accordance
> with the way things should live. These sensations happened too when he
> was working in the fields. Sometimes the sun burned into him so he raised
> his back and tried to look at it, knowing there was power and bigness there.[4]

Barratt outlines the protagonist's development from an Indian youngster at the beginning of *A Brighter Sun* to a mature young West Indian
man who assumes political responsibility at the end of *Turn Again Tiger*.
In the attempt to find a place for himself in a racially divided and amorphous society, Tiger clearly loses some of his links with his Indian heritage. The critical consensus has, however, tended to simplify Selvon's approach to creolisation, sometimes instigated by Selvon's own comments
on his creolised background. Simon Gikandi, for instance, concludes that

> few Caribbean writers have posited creolisation as a metacode for West
> Indian society as much as Selvon... Instead of seeking the sources of his
> writing in the rich Indian heritage that East Indians in Trinidad have
> sustained in the plantation, Selvon has relegated such tradition to back-
> ground and local colour, moving beyond them to assert the liberating
> potential of creolisation.[6]

However, Barratt points out that creolisation for Tiger does not result
in the total disintegration of his Indianness. For Barratt, Tiger seems rather
to be aiming for a West Indian identity which does not assimilate, but in-
corporates, his Indian being. This is eventually achieved in *Turn Again*

Tiger, where the protagonist returns to the cane fields, and symbolically to the historical past of his Indian ancestors, and manages to rid himself of his obsessions and anxieties conditioned by the colonial past.

Barratt's reading of *A Brighter Sun* suggests that there, too, Selvon's depiction of creolisation is much more ambivalent, and that the Indian heritage has a stronger presence in the novel than Gikandi's reading allows, or Selvon himself was sometimes willing to admit. For instance, on the surface, the first visit of Tiger's family to Barataria appears to offer a clash between their mean spirited ethnic exclusiveness and Tiger's open minded creoleness, particularly when his family express their misgivings about Tiger's cordial friendship with his Black neighbours, Joe and Rita:

> 'Is only nigger friend you makeam since you come?' his *bap* asked. 'Plenty Indian liveam dis side. Is true them is good neighbour, but you must look for Indian friend, like you and you wife. Indian must keep together.'
> ...
> 'What you bap say is right thing, though,' his uncle said. 'Nigger people all right, but you must let creole keep they distance. You too young to know these things, but I older than you. Allyuh better make Indian friend.'[7]

But, though on the surface Selvon parodies Tiger's father's and uncle's argument that 'Indian must keep together' as being old style 'coolie' ways, other events in the novel and the trajectory of *Turn Again Tiger* suggest that these long-established strategies for survival, in part shaped by the tensions between the African and Indian communities, cannot be disposed of so easily. As David Dabydeen has maintained:

> For over three hundred years Africans have been coerced into labour under terrible conditions and with enormous losses of life. It was largely their labour which created profitable colonial enterprises, and they saw little of the rewards for themselves. Freedom from slavery saw a resolve never to be dominated again by other ethnic groups. From the very beginning of the indentureship period, Indians were perceived as a threat to African security, a threat to adequate wages and other material resources.[8]

Another aspect of the ambiguity of Selvon's treatment of Tiger's creolisation manifests itself when he shows Tiger becoming obsessed with the power of literacy; books 'about England and America' being his prime focus of interest. Selvon is not without irony here, as, for the illiterate Tiger, reading seems to be inevitably linked to the exotic, i.e. 'white' texts.

Selvon subtly hints here at one trap creolisation may pose, if one does not begin the journey with a consciousness of the value of one's cultural roots. The sense of entrapment is reinforced when Tiger resorts to memorising words and their definitions from the dictionary and blindly participates in the construction of the Churchill-Roosevelt Highway, a symbol of American imperialism. This phase of his life marks a temporary aliena-tion from his wife, family and ethnic background. Unlike his friends in the village, he is willing to give up his garden and work for the American construction company, as the attraction of making money and 'progress' is alluring: 'He had no intention of continuing to farm the land.'⁹ At these stages in Tiger's individuation, creolisation becomes pure mimicry.

But, as Barratt points out, particularly through his relationship with old Sookdeo, Tiger begins a process of return, so that at the end of the novel, Selvon has Tiger gazing up at the sky and muttering: 'Now is a good time to plant corn'. To conclude, there is still scope for further critical assessment of Selvon's perspectives on ethnicity, creolisation and the rela-tionship between the Indian cultural heritage and what it means to be West Indian.

After the sad and notorious occasion at the Commonwealth Institute in 1986 when Selvon was slapped by an angry Black woman over the al-leged sexism of his treatment of women in his fiction, Paola Loreto's es-say 'The Male Mind and the Female Heart: Selvon's Ways to Knowledge in the "Tiger Books"' is a timely and coolly balanced assessment of Selvon's treatment of gender. Loreto scrutinises the role of women in *A Brighter Sun* and *Turn Again Tiger*, and addresses the widely held belief that the female characters in Selvon are merely objects of desire. She argues that in Selvon's portrayal of Tiger and Urmilla, there is an implicit attribution of complementary ways of looking for wisdom and meaning in the indi-vidual's existence. While Tiger's way to knowledge leads him to valuing book learning, Urmilla's – and Barataria's other women's – way is directed by her instincts. According to Loreto, for Urmilla knowledge is not the fruit of disembodied rationalising. Awareness comes to her through the sensations arising in her body from the metamorphosis of motherhood. In this respect, Urmilla's position connects to the values of land, of plant-ing and growing (the Indian values in the novel that Tiger has to redis-cover). Loreto does, however, suggest that while Selvon gives male and female psychologies of knowledge equal credit, there is in the writing a closer identification with the male point of view, compared to a more vaguely expressed longing for the female perspective. Loreto's contribution is a pioneering one and there is further scope for study of the female characters in his novels, in particular a reading of the women against the background of an Indian aesthetic.

Ever since the publication of *A Brighter Sun* critical attention has been directed at Selvon's use of dialect: the consciously crafted Caribbean or Trinidad creole, an innovation in West Indian literature which managed to 'bridge the gap between the teller of the tale and the tale itself... marking an important departure from the more inflexible and standard modes of portraying black or peasant characters in English fiction'.[5]

Maureen Warner-Lewis's essay 'Sam Selvon's Linguistic Extravaganza: *Moses Ascending*' takes the discussion of Selvon's use of language beyond a simple notion of democratisation. What she shows is just how innovative, how artfully literary *and* democratic Selvon was in his inspired play with language. She locates her analysis both in the way Selvon creates the character of Moses through the language he uses in his supposed memoirs, and in the way that Selvon's intertextual play with language registers creates a complex and ironic relationship between Caribbean writing and the Western literary tradition. At one level Moses's language use reflects the perils of the West Indian immigrant's acculturation to the mother country. Moses's aspirations to gentility and landlordship are paralleled on the linguistic plane, as he attempts to impress the potential readers with his masterful handling of the Queen's English: 'I will knock them in the Old Kent Road with my language alone... My very usage of English will have them rolling in the aisles.'[12] Warner-Lewis thoroughly scrutinises Moses's language and uncovers a mix of various linguistic registers that swiftly shift within the text, the incongruity of language codes and inconsistent grammatical forms. Selvon, who is, of course, wholly knowing, shows Moses as at once knowing and naïve. Moses as supposed writer of his memoirs sometimes consciously creates humour for his readers by these means, yet his stylistic variations are not always controlled and he sometimes falls victim to his own eclecticism, flamboyance, and striving for effect. So, according to Warner-Lewis, at one level this linguistic hybridisation and extravaganza characterises Moses's marginal status as a migrant, as an outsider, and reveals the fluctuations attendant on his tenuous social and economic position, and his desire for upward class mobility. At another level,

Warner-Lewis shows Selvon as a highly conscious literary artist engaging in a subversive dialogue with the Western literary tradition, very far removed from the sentimental stereotype of 'Sam' as the simple, comic entertainer.

The focus on Selvon's literariness and the structure of ideas in his work (reminding us that the young Sam Selvon saw himself as a philosopher as well as a novelist) is extended in John Thieme's essay '"The World Turn Upside Down": Carnival Patterns in *The Lonely Londoners*'. John Thieme reads the novel in the light of Bakhtinian carnival theory, drawing the conclusion that *The Lonely Londoners* is the seminal West Indian carnival text since it combines an oral narrative voice with the parodic, egalitarian and subversive comedy of Bakhtinian carnival. Thieme develops his argument by comparing *The Lonely Londoners* with V. S. Naipaul's *Miguel Street*. Although in both texts calypso themes and allusions can be discerned, it is the former that achieves the carnivalesque effect. The crucial difference between the two stems from the distinctive West Indian narrative mode that is integral to *The Lonely Londoners*. According to Thieme, in collapsing the distance between the literary tradition and the oral culture of the protagonists, Selvon subverts the norms of the dominant tradition of Western fiction. Yet, Thieme is well aware that the novel does not simply celebrate carnival values. Although these values help the characters to cope with their life in London, the boys' lifestyle, based on 'oldtalk', may also be read as a form of self-evasion.

In his reluctance to talk about his work or his social and political views (except on the rarest of occasions), Selvon carefully maintained the ambivalences of his dramatisation of the Caribbean condition. But ambivalences are rarely balanced, and the essays by Victor J. Ramraj, Ken Ramchand and John Stephen Martin take up revealingly different positions on where they think Selvon stood in relation to the world he dramatises. Victor J. Ramraj's 'The Philosophy of Neutrality' focuses on the Moses-Galahad relationship and the two protagonists' different forms of political commitment in *Moses Ascending* and *Moses Migrating*. In both novels, Selvon pokes fun at the politically militant. In *Moses Ascending* Galahad's transformation into a Black Power activist is satirised by Selvon through Moses's observations. Conversely, Moses is ridiculed by Galahad for his apolitical stance; later Moses's brief and naïve flirtation with political activism comically reveals the hollowness of his commitments.

Politics, radical or otherwise, are chiefly the opportunity for tricksters and their scams. In *Moses Migrating* it is Moses himself who becomes politically committed by appointing himself ambassador to Britain, whose purpose on his trip to Trinidad is the promotion of British culture. Here, Selvon's satire is not directed through Moses but against him. Ramraj contrasts the way that in *Moses Ascending* and *Moses Migrating* Moses and Galahad in a sense cancel each other out, with *The Lonely Londoners* where the Moses-Galahad relationship can be seen to reflect the classic dichotomy of the writer's psyche (the sedentary observer and the active participant), with Galahad functioning as Moses's *alter ego*. Ramraj concludes that in *Moses Migrating* the polarised aspects of Moses's psyche have finally come together, as Moses is now as cavalier and activist as Galahad.

In his essay 'Comedy as Evasion in the Later Novels of Sam Selvon', which he revised for this book, Kenneth Ramchand takes a highly critical stance towards *Moses Ascending* and, to a greater extent, *Moses Migrating*. Apart from regretting the loss of the introspective and questioning character – for him a most precious feature of Selvon's early novels – Ramchand criticises the imbalance between tragedy and comedy in the later Moses novels. In *The Lonely Londoners* comedy was based upon certain kinds of inconsistencies in the West Indian protagonists' behaviour in the alien London society; the tragedy is brought to the fore most explicitly in the famous 'Under the kiff-kiff laughter' passage at the end of the novel. In this novel, tragedy and comedy are inseparable, different faces of the same coin. This healthy balance, according to Ramchand, is not consistently maintained in the sequels. Instead, the comedy moves to a vein of farce or burlesque, evoking a cynicism or an agnosticism which can mock all sides of every question. In his reading of *Moses Ascending* Ramchand suggests that Moses's function is more important than his character, which results in a confusing Moses, one who is highly situational, self-deceiving and pretentious, whose actions are seldom consistent. For the reader, Ramchand argues, it becomes difficult, therefore, to establish his character by attributing to him qualities that appear in the various episodes. Moreover, the serious issues raised in *The Lonely Londoners* are bypassed. With regard to *Moses Migrating*, Ramchand goes a step further, suggesting that a crisis is reached, that Selvon is unable either to settle into a tone appropriate to Moses's emotional impasse or to re-establish an appearance of harmony after the text's revelation of the emptiness, bad faith and confusion in

Moses's life. Ramchand concludes that the challenge of the situation Selvon has created is not met by the ending that he uses to close off the work. Ramchand believes that there are convincing traces in the novel of a Moses who could have stayed on the island with Doris. He further speculates not only on the extent to which Moses is shown as being evasive, but also wonders whether Selvon is using comedy as a means of evasion, rather than, as in *The Lonely Londoners*, as part of a vision that sees the comic and the tragic as two sides of the same coin. Ramchand's approach takes Selvon seriously as a philosophical writer, but finds the two later Moses novels wanting in comparison to the subtlety of *The Lonely Londoners*. In repressing the tragic vision of the latter, the two later novels, according to Ramchand, deny the possibility of harmony and balance.

Whereas Ramraj's and Ramchand's essays question the notion that the three Moses books constitute a proper trilogy on the grounds of inconsistencies in character development and divergent narrative strategies, the last essay of this book, 'The Odyssey of Sam Selvon's Moses' by John Stephen Martin, argues for the existence of three truly consecutive texts. Martin focuses on Moses's journeyings, which span more than thirty years and lead from Trinidad to the mother country, from England to Trinidad and back again to England. His argument takes as its starting point Ramchand's dictum that Selvon is a philosophical writer. According to Martin it is this philosophical element that transforms Moses's life from a failed journey to 'a promised land' into an odyssey about coming home to one's self. While Selvon subtly parodies the biblical Moses in the first two novels, in *Moses Migrating* the irony is directed at Moses's Odysseus-like attempt to return to his Trinidad home after almost three decades of subtle anglicisation.

Martin's essay, along with most of the essays in this volume, has a good deal to say about the frequent recourse to allusion to seminal Western texts in Selvon's work. It has been noted by many critics that in some of his work Selvon subverts or at least makes play with the Western literary tradition. Amongst other critical assessments, two essays by Helen Tiffin on *Moses Ascending* come to mind, in which Selvon's employment of counter-discursive strategies is celebrated.[13] However, there appears to be a type of literary allusion and intertextuality in Selvon's prose that exists outside the notion of the 'empire writing back' (by inverting or rewriting such crucial motifs as the Prospero-Caliban or the Crusoe-Friday relationship).

Several of the essays reveal Selvon's prose as an echo chamber of Western literary texts, carrying such philosophical archetypes as the quest, which are quintessentially part of the tradition and which are not subverted. In this regard, a reading of *The Lonely Londoners* against *The Quest of the Holy Grail* as well as the *Bible* would seem instructive.

The notion of the quest, echoing the chivalrous adventures in the Arthurian legend across a land strewn with fantastic danger and false promises, connect together the various episodes concerning the 'boys' in Selvon's novel. There is, of course, Sir Galahad, as the newcomer, Henry Oliver, is dubbed by Moses. The quest of Selvon's Galahad in London might not be for the Holy Grail but, along with the rest of the boys, he is searching for something just as elusive: acceptance in the mother country. Like a hot-headed tyro knight, Galahad rejects the tentative instructions offered by the knowing veteran Moses, proudly believing that he can do without the latter's help. As soon as Galahad heads for the tube station, 'a feeling of loneliness and fright come on him all of a sudden. He forget all the brave words he was talking to Moses... The sun shining. But Galahad never see the sun look like how it looking now. No heat from it, it just there in the sky like a force-ripe orange.'[14] Moses, having been through this kind of experience years ago, seems to have expected the novice knight's failure and waits behind the street corner. Galahad is more than happy when Moses reappears. '"Moses," he say. "I too glad to see you boy. If you don't mind I want you to come with me."'[15] The episode shows close yet ironic intertextuality with a passage in *The Quest of the Holy Grail*, when Galahad's newly appointed knight with similarly bold pride, thinks he is capable of taking a different road from his adviser and fails accordingly. 'At once the enemy pierced you with one of his darts. Shall I tell you which? It was the dart of pride.'[16]

Then there is Bart's quest for his beloved Beatrice, whose name and irrecoverable loss in the novel alludes to Dante's heroine in *Divina Commedia*.[17] Selvon gives the word play another twist: Bart not only echoes the Dantian quest for the beloved woman that, in *The Lonely Londoners*, leaves him 'haggard and haunted', but also once more the Arthurian legend. Bart is, of course, a short form for Arthur.

The analogy with *The Quest of the Holy Grail* resurfaces at the end of *The Lonely Londoners* during Moses's epiphanic moment standing on the banks of the Thames. Although Moses's profound realisation does not yield him spiritual communion with God, as is the case with Galahad in the Arthurian legend, Moses's experience is equally metaphysical. He may not have led his people to 'the promised land', yet in the moment of elation with its 'greatness and vastness' he gains a consciousness that enables him to narrate the story of his tribe. As Chris Campbell suggests, Moses's face-to-face encounter with the Thames and the motif of power personified in the river as the defender of the host country's shores, which drowns or accepts invaders, is also to be found in the river Tiber in Book VIII of Virgil's *Aeneid* and in the Trojan river Xanthos in Book XXI of Homer's *The Iliad*.[18] The allusion to Virgil is further reinforced as both heroes, Aeneas and Moses, are equally unsuccessful in establishing the hoped-for nation.

Even though the biblical echo of Moses's name has been played down by Selvon, the thematic parallels between *The Lonely Londoners* and the *Bible* can be seen in the notions of the exodus and the promised land, which cannot be entered by Moses and his fellow West Indians. And, like his biblical namesake, Moses has not only become the appointed leader of his tribe, but 'a cross-bearer' as well: 'Sometimes listening to them, he look in each face, and he feel a great compassion for every one of them, as if he live each of their lives, one by one, and all the strain and stress come to rest on his shoulders.'[19] As Gordon Rohlehr has pointed out, 'Moses at the end of the book has a high priest's role… he becomes a repository for group consciousness, a sort of archetypal old man, a Teresias figure.'[20] And, like the biblical Moses, Selvon's hero becomes jaded with his role and sad-dened by the condition of his people.[21]

Ramraj's essay comes to a similar kind of conclusion when he locates Moses's now more solitary quest in Arthurian archetype. He suggests that there has been a merging of Moses's and Galahad's personas, and points to Selvon's parallel between Moses's Carnival prize and Galahad's find-ing of the Holy Grail in the Arthurian legend. His essay suggests, too, that these parallels go beyond parody (though they contain elements of it) or 'writing back' to a quite unironic location of Moses's situation in the resonant archetypes to be found in the Arthurian legend. The ending at Heathrow Airport in *Moses Migrating* epitomises Moses's state of total exile, and reads even more tragically when Moses's epiphanic moment on the banks of the Thames is brought back to mind. That moment of elation, with an almost heroically composed Moses looking down the Thames,

England's symbolic gateway to empire, stands in dramatic contrast to the final scene at Heathrow, the country's twentieth-century gate to the world. In the earlier novel, Moses is part of the tribe, part of the 'round table' of the boys. At the end of *Moses Migrating,* he is on his own, like the lonely knight in pursuit of the grail. The ending is multilayered. In the terms of the realistic novel it shows Moses paying for his bad faith and duplicity by losing both companionship and a spot of earth he can call his own. In terms of parody, it shows a stranded Moses who has become a mere caricature of his former self, 'still playing charade':[22]

> 'Hold on,' I say, and open my plastic carrier bag and take out the silver cup first prize what I get in Trinidad for my loyal impersonation of Britannia. 'I have this to declare,' and hold it up, like Arthur Ashe hold up the Wimbledon Cup when he win the tennis, for all the peoples in the airport to see. Only to me it was like holding up the Holy Grail.[23]

But the ending also suggests that Selvon was using the literary echoes to say something about a deeper human truth. Thus, Moses's desperate yielding to the spirit of Britannia gains its full impact when juxtaposed with the literary source it echoes, *The Quest of the Holy Grail.* There Galahad recognises that the ultimate price of acquiring the Holy Grail is to yield his spirit to God:

> Lord, I worship Thee and give thanks that Thou hast granted my desire, for now I see revealed what tongue could not relate nor heart conceive. Here is the source of valour undismayed, the spring-head of endeavour; here I see the wonder that passes every other! And since, sweet Lord, Thou hast fulfilled my wish to let me see what I have ever craved, I pray Thee now that in this state Thou suffer me to pass from earthly life to eternal.[24]

To sum up, Sam Selvon's fiction does indeed make play with the imposed Western culture, i.e. English literature and the older Western literatures that have flowed into it, but, at the same time, it pays tribute to the very same tradition by revelling in the large reservoir of its achievements. No doubt, further critical exploration of these intertextual relationships will show that Selvon's oeuvre still has many treasures to offer. It is to be hoped that in the future the critical scope will be extended to Selvon's less studied novels as well as to his short fiction, and, last but not least, to his radio plays, some of which have been made available in book form.[25]

   This book concludes with two interviews conducted, respectively, by John Thieme and Alessandra Dotti. In the first Selvon talks about his early steps as a writer in the 1950s and about how the BBC programme, *Caribbean Voices*, produced by Henry Swanzy, got his career started. Further topics for conversation are Selvon's move to Canada after twenty-eight years of living in England, his London novels and the shift in narrative strategies between *The Lonely Londoners* and *Moses Ascending*. In Dotti's interview, Selvon's love for London and the English countryside, as evoked by the poetry of Wordsworth and Keats, is brought to the fore. She also tries to shed light on the role of women in Selvon's novel's. She takes a different stance from Paola Loreto's essay, confronting Selvon with the view that the female characters are mere objects of desire. The bibliography at the end of the book gives an overview of Sam Selvon's oeuvre as well as of the critical work so far published.

1 Kenneth Ramchand, 'A Brighter Sun', in *An Introduction to the Study of West Indian Literature* (London: Nelson, 1976), pp.58-72.

2 Roydon Salick, 'Introduction', in *A Brighter Sun*, by Sam Selvon (Harlow, Essex: Longman, 1992).

3 Clem Seecharan, *Tiger in the Stars: The Anatomy of Indian Achievement in British Guiana 1919-1929* (London: Macmillan, 1997), p.158.

4 Sam Selvon, *A Brighter Sun* (Harlow, Essex: Longman, 1985), p.64.

5 Susheila Nasta (ed.), *Critical Perspectives on Sam Selvon* (Washington, D.C.: Three Continents Press, 1988), pp.7-8.

6 Simon Gikandi, 'Beyond the *Kala-pani*: The Trinidad Novels of Samuel Selvon', in *Writing in Limbo: Modernism and Caribbean Literature* (Ithaca and London: Cornell University Press, 1992), p.111.

7 Selvon, *A Brighter Sun*, pp.47-48.

8 David Dabydeen, 'Preface', in *India in the Caribbean*, ed. by David Dabydeen and Brinsley Samaroo (London: Hansib, 1987), pp.10-11.

9 Selvon, *A Brighter Sun*, p.118.

10 Ramchand, p.70.

11 Selvon, *A Brighter Sun*, p.198.

12 Sam Selvon, *Moses Ascending* (Oxford: Heinemann, 1975), p.78.

13 Helen Tiffin, 'Post-Colonial Literatures and Counter-Discourse', *Kunapipi*, 9:3 (1987), pp.17-33. And with particular focus on *Moses Ascending* and *Moses Migrating*: '"Under the Kiff-Kiff Laughter": Stereotype and Subversion in *Moses Ascending* and *Moses Migrating*', in *Tiger's Triumph: Celebrating Sam Selvon*, ed. by Susheila Nasta and Anna Rutherford (London: Dangaroo Press, 1995), pp.130-139. See also Edward Baugh, 'Belittling the Great Tradition, in Good Humour', in *The Comic Vision in West Indian Literature*, ed. by Roydon Salick (San Fernando: Printex, 1988), pp.1-9.

14 Sam Selvon, *The Lonely Londoners* (Harlow, Essex: Longman, 1985), p.42.

15 Ibid., p.43.

16 *The Quest of the Holy Grail*, transl. by P. M. Matarasso (London: Penguin, 1969), p.71.

17 As Nick Wong has remarked, however, it is actually the shorter but nonetheless significant *Vita Nova* that appears to have the strongest affinities to *The Lonely Londoners*, for it is in that series of meditations

on love that Dante speaks about fathoming the significance of his relationship with Beatrice and about the changes that occur upon her loss. See Nick Wong, 'Alienation, Fantasy and Literary Awakening in London: A Comparative Consideration of Sam Selvon's *The Lonely Londoners* and S. I. Martin's *Incomparable World*' (Unpublished Master's Paper, University of Warwick, 4 May 2000).

18 Chris Campbell, 'Equiano's Odyssey: Reconceptualising the Epic' (Unpublished Master's Dissertation, University of Warwick, 1999).

19 Selvon, *The Lonely Londoners*, p.139.

20 Gordon Rohlehr, 'Samuel Selvon and the Language of the People', in *Critics on Caribbean Literature*, ed. by Edward Baugh (London: George Allen & Unwin, 1978), pp.160-161.

21 See Margaret Paul Joseph, *Caliban in Exile: The Outsider in Caribbean Fiction* (New York: Greenwood, 1992), p.111, footnote 10.

22 Sam Selvon, *Moses Migrating* (Washington, D.C.: Three Continents Press, 1992), p.179.

23 Ibid., p.179.

24 *The Quest of the Holy Grail*, p.283.

25 Sam Selvon, *Eldorado West One*, ed. and introd. by Susheila Nasta (Leeds: Peepal Tree Press, 1988); and *Highway in the Sun and Other Plays* (Leeds: Peepal Tree Press, 1991).

SAM SELVON'S TIGER:
IN SEARCH OF SELF-AWARENESS

HAROLD BARRATT

Although the decades before the 1950s produced important writers – Herbert George de Lisser, C. L. R. James, Alfred Mendes, and Edgar Mittelholzer, for instance – a substantial body of distinctive and distinguished West Indian literature, the kind produced by novelists and poets such as V. S. Naipaul, Derek Walcott, Wilson Harris, and George Lamming, all of them writers of the first order, was yet to come. By the end of the sixties Naipaul had already written some ten books, including the brilliant *A House for Mr. Biswas* and *The Loss of El Dorado*; Lamming's *In the Castle of My Skin*, Harris's Guiana Quartet, several collections of Walcott's poems, and six of Sam Selvon's novels had also appeared.

The Indian diaspora from the Gangetic plain contributed 143,939 indentured workers to Trinidad from 1845 to 1917, when the last boatload of largely agricultural workers arrived. By 1871 Indians had become the backbone of the sugar industry and made up some 25 percent of Trinidad's population. Of this number 4,545 were locally born.[1] Sam Selvon is a product of this monumental diaspora, which altered, profoundly and permanently, Trinidad's economic, social, and cultural complexion. Selvon, born in Trinidad in 1923 of an Indian dry goods merchant and a half-Scottish, half-Indian mother, is one of those distinguished writers who contributed to the remarkable emergence of a vibrant West Indian literature in the fifties and sixties. In his London fiction Selvon explores with sensitivity and perception, and a humour brilliantly mixed with pathos, the vicissitudes of the largely unskilled, displaced West Indians who are merely surviving in a hostile society that does not welcome them and confines them to menial jobs.[2] None of Selvon's expatriate West Indians, including the charismatic Moses, who functions as the group's father and mentor and whose withers have long since been wrung through the London mill, feels that he belongs in Mother England, the promised land for all good colonials. The three novels and the short stories that comprise the London fiction, together with *A Brighter Sun* (1952) and *Turn Again Tiger* (1958), guarantee Selvon a permanent place in the history of West Indian literature.

A Brighter Sun can of course be read and appreciated separately from its sequel, *Turn Again Tiger*; since, however, the internalising of Tiger's identity, which is the central focus of *A Brighter Sun*, is continued and indeed consolidated in the sequel, it is appropriate, and certainly rewarding, to study both novels together.

A Brighter Sun is a historically important work because of Selvon's use of Trinidadian dialect. It would appear that his use of the dialect was not a studied stylistic device, since he has said that he 'did not even know the full meaning of the word dialect' when he wrote the novel. He was more concerned with 'the translation of the emotions, feelings and situations than with reproducing a historically accurate language. If I find a language form that works,' he added, 'I will use it.'[3] *A Brighter Sun* is also a pivotal novel because its central theme is the main character's quest for what has become the most compelling issue in West Indian literature: identity, self-awareness and wholeness in a colonial and pluralistic society infected with a good deal of self-contempt, and still showing the psychic scars of slavery and the equally dehumanising indenture system.

Selvon drew his portrait of Tiger from his acquaintance with an old Indian man of the same name who symbolised for him 'the young peasant who starts off by gradually discovering about life'. The old man's voyage of discovery, one may suppose, also served as the catalyst for the two novels, and indeed may have helped to shape Selvon's philosophy: 'You have to discover yourself, then only can you be of some use to humanity.'[4] *A Brighter Sun* is a careful and uncommonly sensitive examination of the growing sensibilities of an Indian youngster who is suddenly wrenched from the canefields of Chaguanas, where many of the indentured Indian workers settled, and the security of parents and playmates and finds himself a married man having to fend for two people in Barataria, a considerably more complex community a few miles outside of Port of Spain, Trinidad's bristling capital. At first Tiger is a clumsy innocent who is ignorant to the point of stupidity and blindly obedient to his parents' wishes. Even though he is married, he is of course still a child, and his urge to return to the protection of the womb when life becomes too problematic is not surprising. And his idea of manhood is adolescent: 'Men smoked: he would smoke.'[5] At the same time one can discern in Tiger a potential for growth and wisdom. As he and his wife Urmilla, who is equally young and callow, begin to establish the basis of a life together, they are prematurely confronted by adult responsibilities; and Tiger gradually rejects the adolescent philosophy, 'all of we is Indian,' and replaces it with a tentative self-assertiveness, as well as a social and political awareness and a restless urge to enlarge the horizons of his limited education. For instance, shortly after his arrival in Barataria he must negotiate for two lots of land. The transaction is at first disconcerting, and he 'wished his father or one of his uncles was there with him'. But this desire, Selvon writes, 'made him ashamed. He was married, and he was a big man now. He might as well learn to do things without the assistance of other people' (13). Meanwhile, racially mixed Barataria gives Tiger the opportunity to broaden his relationship with blacks and other ethnic groups. Three of these neighbours, Joe, Rita, and old Sookdeo, are particularly important in Tiger's education. Old Sookdeo, an eccentric but deceptively wise Indian, says to Tiger, 'Haveam some ting yuh learn only by experience' (78). Tiger learns from experience that manhood does not mean possessing a wife and fathering a child; nor does it mean smoking and drinking rum. Manhood means awareness of one's identity as a unique individual; it also means satisfying one's hunger for knowledge. In one of his many brooding soliloquies Tiger asks, 'Ain't a man is a man, don't mind if he skin not white, or if he hair curl?' (48). But this new-found wisdom is abhorrent to Tiger's parents, for whom the preservation of their son's Indian identity is mandatory, and they are shocked by Tiger's friendship with Joe and Rita, whose blackness threatens to creolise their son. As Tiger's perceptions mature, as his experiences become increasingly complex, he eventually recognises that 'it was what you was inside that count' (204).

Several factors contribute to Tiger's social and political awakening. Of these, his day-to-day experiences, especially his relationship with the non-

Indian members of cosmopolitan Barataria, are important factors in his growing consciousness. Two of these experiences are particularly enlightening. Tiger's humiliating encounter with a salesgirl in a fashionable Port of Spain store is instructive. When she ignores him and waits on a white woman instead, Tiger, who had believed that his Indianness gave him at least second-class status in the island's racial hierarchy, discovers that in the eyes of those for whom whiteness is the ultimate measure of excellence, Indian and black are equally unimportant. The second experience is equally, if not more, disconcerting and traumatic. When, during a rainstorm, he tries to get medical aid for Urmilla, the Indian and black doctors give his pleas for help short and rude shrift. But an English doctor from Port of Spain's elite St. Clair district comes to Urmilla's aid. The experience teaches him that good and evil are everywhere, and, furthermore, that people are neither black nor white, only grey. And there is more: Tiger is forced to consider the possibility that the 'wite man must always laugh at we coloured people, because we so stupid' (189). The next day Tiger confronts the Indian and black doctors and verbally abuses them in the presence of patients and onlookers. His anger is partly displaced, and it is certainly fuelled by his sense of shame and guilt for his brutal treatment of Urmilla after the dinner scene with the two Americans. Muzzy with drink, Tiger attacks the pregnant Urmilla, who, wishing to please his guests, has put on makeup and instead of obsequiously withdrawing to the kitchen, which she had tried to do at the start of the evening's entertainment, has a drink at the insistence of the Americans. This is too much for Tiger, to whom Urmilla looks 'like a whore in Port of Spain' (175); and when he kicks his pregnant and defenceless wife in the face and stomach, it is undoubtedly the nadir of his young life. But Tiger's anger also brings to the surface issues that have been subconsciously troubling him: What is the connection between individual and national integrity? How can the island achieve national independence in the absence of individual integrity? In the encounters with the salesgirl and the doctors a seed has been planted, and it will eventually grow into Tiger's nagging desire for personal and, later on, national identity.

Tiger's questions and anxieties about the need for national independence point to his growing maturity, and they match his own hunger for personal independence and identity. One thinks here of his desire, notwithstanding some initial anxiety, to strike out on his own as soon as he has arrived in Barataria; and not too long after his confrontation with the doctors Tiger asks Joe: 'But listen, it ain't have a way how we could govern weself? Ain't it have a thing call self-government?' (196). Tiger's questions and conversations with Joe emphasise his growing preoccupation with self-awareness. His confusion and doubts are not unlike Selvon's. In more than one interview Selvon has betrayed his strong sense of displacement. In an interview with Peter Nazareth, Selvon refers more than once to his rootlessness, to his sense of being a displaced writer, as well as the amorphousness of his identity.[6] Unlike his compatriot V. S. Naipaul, Selvon did not grow up in the sort of closed yet disintegrating Hindu world Naipaul has described more than once.

It is not surprising that rootlessness is a strong theme in Selvon's *An Island Is a World* (1955) and *I Hear Thunder* (1963), which have been unfortunately neglected, but nonetheless aid one's understanding of *A Brighter Sun*. Both novels are finely focused and accurate pictures of Trinidad society in the forties and fifties. It is a society of petty racism, with men and women lost in the void of colonial neglect, the kind of society with which Selvon is intimately familiar and from which he himself escaped. Many of the characters in these novels, such as Adrian and Mark of *I Hear Thunder* and the Indian men of *An Island Is a World*, are complex and fully embodied; and Selvon's best female portraits can be found in both novels. The Indian characters resemble Tiger to the extent that they are ready to philosophise at the slightest encouragement. Like Tiger, they are also introspective and melancholy. More important, they too are seeking some sort of fulfilling wholeness. Foster, 'the lost soul groping in the dark',[7] is cabined, cribbed, and confined by his island home, and he desperately flees Trinidad in search of fulfilment in London. But the promised land only exacerbates his alienation and hopelessness. Rufus, Foster's brother, also flees Trinidad and a loveless marriage for America's greener pastures. His search ends in failure and bigamy. Although he has lived, raised a family, and prospered in Trinidad for several years, Johnny, the Indian jeweller whose daughters Foster and Rufus marry, stubbornly regards India as his spiritual home. Becoming increasingly alienated from his family, to say nothing of the frustration he suffers when he fails to achieve his eccentric goal of harnessing the force of gravity, he turns to excessive drinking and then to the government's plan to return disaffected Indians to Mother India. But even as he departs for India, Nehru, to whom the disaffected have written for support, responds with no encouragement and indeed sees no place for Johnny and the other victims of the diaspora in postcolonial India.

While he struggles to find a significant place in his racially divisive and amorphous society, to say nothing of trying to understand the place of his seemingly insignificant island in the world, Tiger loses some of his links with his tenuous Indian heritage. Tiger's increasing creolisation, however, does not mean the total disintegration of his Indianness. The experiences of Pariag, the Indian outcast in Earl Lovelace's *The Dragon Can't Dance*, will point a useful comparison. Pariag abandons the narrowness of a predominantly Indian sugar estate and dependence upon an overbearing uncle for Port of Spain, 'where people could see him, and he could be somebody in their eyes'.[8] He, too, is in search of an awareness beyond that of Indian and black; but the dominant black community of Calvary Hill, where he and his wife have come to live, rejects them out of hand. Pariag's Indianness makes him an interloper. He is deliberately excluded from the Christmas festivities and, more important, the Carnival celebration, the community's central ritual, which is a complex amalgam of rebellion, fantasy, drama, and escapism and a symbolic embodiment of the quest for identity. Pariag experiences a symbolic crucifixion on Calvary Hill – a crucifixion adumbrated in Lovelace's skilful use of Ash Wednesday imagery and the farcical crucifixion of a religious crackpot at the start of the novel – when his neighbours, convinced that his purchase of a new bicycle is his attempt to rise above 'the equalness of everybody' (103), smash the machine to pieces. Lovelace, however, turns Pariag's symbolic death into a victory and rebirth, for his stoic acceptance of his victimisation makes him 'alive and a person' to his hostile neighbours. The symbolic crucifixion, furthermore, is said to be 'a sacred moment for it joined people together to a sense of their humanness and beauty' (141).

This sense of a primal, inviolable humanness, a theme also noticeable in Lovelace's *The Wine of Astonishment*, is implicit in Tiger's desire for an identity that transcends racial divisions. Put another way, Tiger seems to be aiming for a West Indian identity that would not assimilate, but incorporate, his Indian being. Tiger's relatives are products of the diaspora, displaced in a disconcertingly pluralistic society; and they are ferociously Hindu: 'Nigger people all right, but you must let creole keep they distance,' his uncle advises (48). Tiger has been spawned by this threatened

Hindu world; but he is also palpably West Indian. He is indeed an early West Indian hero whose quest for integrity and personal independence is a reflection of the individual's desire to overcome the colonial neglect so deeply embedded in the West Indian psyche, the sort of syndrome that bears some resemblance to George Lamming's term 'psychic shame'.[9]

Lamming has emphasised Selvon's importance as an explorer of the social situation in the West Indies, and he has drawn attention to the peasant roots of Selvon's fiction.[10] But Lamming does not discuss the intimate bond between Selvon's peasants and the land they cultivate. Some commentators, unfortunately, have given Tiger's bond with the land short shrift; recognition of this bond, however, is essential for an understanding of Tiger. It is true that Tiger is indeed happy to give up small farming in order to earn a higher income working with the Americans who are building a road through Barataria; but Tiger's bond with the land is considerably more than a mere economic necessity. The land helps to mould his growing sensibilities, and Selvon emphasises the power of this bond in strategic periods in Tiger's life. Consider, for example, an early period in his life, a time of confusion and bewilderment about the war raging in Europe, a time of doubt about his self-worth and capacity for growth and understanding. All of these anxieties are alleviated when he turns to the land for relief and understanding. Tiger feels, and in fact participates in, the power 'throbbing in the earth, humming in the air, riding the night wind' (113). These moments of communion with the land demonstrate Tiger's abiding love and respect for a power he does not fully comprehend but of which he is nonetheless fully cognisant. Wordsworth and Coleridge, one feels, would have understood Tiger's oneness with the land, sky, and sun. Union with the land, furthermore, gives Tiger the solace he needs and the strength to persevere. 'Whenever big things happen,' he reflects, 'I does go out and look all about, at the birds, at the hills, and the trees, and the sky... And I does get a funny feeling, as if strength coming inside me. That must be God' (117-18). When he rebels against Barataria's narrowness and yearns to escape to the seductive world of Port of Spain, Selvon, we notice, counterpoints this restlessness with Tiger's compelling sensitivity to the land and its fetching nuances.

Two other crucial periods in Tiger's life are worth noting. Although it will provide needed jobs, the building of the road is disruptive and brings uneasiness to Tiger and his neighbours. Immediately, however, Tiger counteracts his anxieties through a simple communion with the land. The second important moment is at the end of the novel. The war in Europe, whose long and devastating arms have also embraced Trinidad, has ended, and Tiger has built a new house. The promise of a sunlit day that he detected in the sky has been realised, we may say. At once Tiger thinks of returning to the canefields of his boyhood; but the thought makes him 'laugh aloud' (215). The laugh signals the end of his innocence, and not a turning away from the land. The novel's final words – "'now is a good time to plant corn," he muttered, gazing up at the sky' (215) – drive this point home. Tiger's words confirm his continuing attraction for the land as the source of an undefined, yet certain, power. Tiger, furthermore, experiences a regeneration in the reaffirmation of his value and the power of the land over his earlier materialistic hunger. Selvon also matches Tiger's bond with the land with his recognition that one pays a price for adulthood: 'It ain't always a man does be able to do the things he want to do' (213). This acceptance of responsibility contrasts sharply with Joe's complacency. Tiger rejects Joe's attitude – 'dey have plenty people who can't write and dey living happy' (42) – out of hand. 'The great distance which separated him from all that was happening' (75) is at the heart of Tiger's restlessness, and the following exchange between Tiger and Joe clearly shows this:

> 'You mean to say, Joe, that you never had ambition to go to college or get a good office job?'
> 'But why, papa? Ah man cud live happy without all dem things.'
> 'Well, Joe, that is you, but as for me, I can't be happy until I find out things.' (111-12)

Tiger's determination to find out more about himself and his world continues in *Turn Again Tiger*. His communion with the land is no less intimate than in the earlier novel. Although he is older and presumably wiser, he still turns to the land for comfort, recognising a superior wisdom in its shifting moods. But the sequel is even more finely focused upon Tiger's quest for self-possession; and the novel has several important links with Selvon's *Those Who Eat the Cascadura* (1972). Both novels explore the vicissitudes of a central Indian character in a tiny and isolated village. Five Rivers, the setting of *Turn Again Tiger*, is a sleepy village where Tiger and his family are temporarily living with his father, who, now that he is foreman at an experimental cane plantation managed by the Englishman Robinson, needs his son's help. Like the bucolic Sans Souci, the setting of *Those Who Eat the Cascadura*, Five Rivers is a microcosm of pre-independent, colonial Trinidad. The three-tiered racial hierarchy, complete with antagonisms and divisiveness, is firmly entrenched at Five Rivers and Sans Souci. There are, however, one or two differences: the social and political centre of Five Rivers is the Chinaman Otto's rumshop, and the village is a more cohesive community than Sans Souci. Racial tension in Five Rivers, moreover, is subordinated to Tiger's quest: 'But when I come a man in truth, I want to possess myself.'[11]

Tiger's continuing hunger for self-possession can be seen in his interminable brooding and deliberately assertive posture in the presence of the formidable Robinson. His assertiveness is all the more noticeable because of its sharp contrast with his father's obsequiousness. Tiger's hunger is effectively dramatised in his violent sexual encounter with Doreen, Robinson's coldly provocative wife. It is the novel's central scene, and it brings to the surface all of Tiger's ambivalence and disingenuousness. Tiger's self-esteem and fragile dignity are shattered when, in a moment of panic, he flees from the sight of Doreen bathing naked in the river. His explanation for his shameful action is glib and disingenuous: 'It had nothing to do with colour or the generation of servility which was behind him. He had fled because she was a woman, a naked woman, and because he was a man' (52). The truth is that Tiger has fled from the bogey of the luscious, forbidden white female, and fear has reduced him, the man 'who drank rum with men and discussed big things like Life and Death' (51), to a terrified, cringing boy. When he does make love to Doreen – it is brutally cold and as ferocious and impersonal as Sarojini's copulation with the Englishman Johnson in *Those Who Eat the Cascadura* – his motives are not as simple as he at first imagined. First, there is the obvious *frisson* of interracial sex, to say nothing of the revenge motive, a feature of the black male-white female syndrome often explored in West Indian literature. There is, too, as Tiger puts it with blunt directness, an even more basic motive: 'I wonder,' he asks himself, 'if under all the old-talk, all I wanted to do was to screw a white woman?' (149). None of these is as important, one feels, as his need to restore his shattered self-esteem and free himself of the paralysing fear of the untouchable but eminently desirable white fruit.

Tiger's frenzied possession of Doreen ought to be read as a symbolic killing. He himself senses this: 'Over here,' he tells Joe when he visits his friend in Barataria, 'some of we still feel white people is God, and that is a hard thing to kill' (158). The possession of Doreen should be set alongside Otto's fight with Singh, who has cuckolded him. The Chinaman must thrash Singh in order to exorcise the jealousy destroying his soul and heal the wound inflicted upon his ego. Tiger must possess Doreen in order to exorcise his own devils. The act brings relief and victory to both men. For Tiger it is the peace he had been subconsciously seeking. Singh's broken hand, meanwhile, can be fixed by a doctor, but Otto 'had to get well inside'. This happens when he conquers 'the hate and jealousy in his heart' (181). Tiger must also come to his own sense of the matter; and he does so with noticeable finality:

> His life had impinged on hers, but only for one purpose. There was no pleasure in the memory for him; afterwards he had shrugged like a snake, changing skins. No triumph, no satisfaction, no extension of desire to make him want to do it again. Just relief, as if he had walked through fire and come out burnt a little, but still very much alive. (180-81)

For Doreen too, the act has been final: she has also rid herself of the twin torments of hate and lust.

If Joe's and Tiger's attitudes toward the encounter with Doreen are compared, its psychological significance for Tiger is at once clear. When he relates the incident, Joe dismisses Tiger's irritating consternation with what appears to be trenchant common sense: 'Men screwing women all over the world every day, Tiger, why you have to make a problem out of this one?' (155). But Tiger sees the incident as a test which he has failed: he has failed to possess himself. Furthermore, he can see in his failure a more universal problem: if Joe is correct and Tiger is merely a drop of water in a river, then he is destined to 'just sit down on his arse and float with the tide' (156); and this destiny Tiger has consistently rejected. Tiger's exorcism is immediately followed by his symbolic purification in the river. A symbolic purification is also suggested after the brutal coupling of Johnson and Sarojini; and here again a comparison with Sarojini's symbolic rape of Johnson will shed some light on Tiger's experience. Sarojini sees union with the Englishman as her highest achievement. But the raping of Johnson is an obvious reversal of the white overseer's raping of

Indian girls in the canefields of Trinidad. Nor does her sexual union with Johnson bring Sarojini any insight or self-awareness. Her childlike dependence upon Johnson is still intact, and at the end of the novel she is a pathetic figure desperately clinging to an obeahman's incantations and rituals and living in the hope of Johnson's unlikely return. Unlike Sarojini, who will never free herself of Johnson – she is carrying his child – Tiger's encounter with Doreen has enlarged his sensibilities, if not matured him. The experience is not unlike the land's continual changes and growth: 'It just like we,' he says of the land; 'we finish one job, and we got to get ready to start another' (181). Tiger's life changes dramatically after the encounter with Doreen: he gives up the crutch of heavy rum-drinking; and the profound change in his life is metaphorically suggested when, walking off the trail one day shortly after the incident, he at once 'righted his direction' (162).

At the end of the novel Tiger comes to terms with his obsessions and anxieties. To this extent he resembles other tormented West Indian heroes, such as Aldrick, the brooding, questing hero of Lovelace's *The Dragon Can't Dance*, whose regeneration is the victory of the self over his escapist fantasies. Unlike men such as Galahad and Battersby, two of Selvon's feckless exiles who are trapped, it would appear, in a permanent stasis, Tiger is driven by a strong sense of purpose, and he achieves an integrity when he realises that he must turn inward to his own inner resources for strength.

---

1 Bridget Brereton, *A History of Modern Trinidad 1783-1962* (London: Heinemann, 1981), p.105.

2 Sam Selvon's London fiction consists of the following: *The Lonely Londoners* (London: Allan Wingate, 1956), *Ways of Sunlight* (London: MacGibbon and Kee, 1957), *The Housing Lark* (London: MacGibbon and Kee, 1965), and *Moses Ascending* (London: Davis-Poynter, 1975).

3 Kenneth Ramchand, 'Sam Selvon Talking: A Conversation with Kenneth Ramchand', in *Critical Perspectives on Sam Selvon*, ed. by Susheila Nasta (Washington: Three Continents Press, 1988), pp.100-101.

4 Michel Fabre, 'Sam Selvon: Interviews and Conversations', ibid., p.69.

5 Sam Selvon, *A Brighter Sun* (London: Longman, 1971), p.11. Subsequent references are cited in the text.

6 Peter Nazareth, 'Interview with Sam Selvon', in *Critical Perspectives*, ed. by Susheila Nasta, op. cit., p.83.

7 Sam Selvon, *An Island Is a World* (London: Allan Wingate, 1955), p.92.

8 Earl Lovelace, *The Dragon Can't Dance* (London: André Deutsch, 1979), p.78. Subsequent references are cited in the text.

9 George Lamming, 'The West Indian People', *New World Quarterly*, 2:2 (1966), p.69.

10 George Lamming, *The Pleasures of Exile* (London: Allison and Busby, 1980), p.45.

11 Sam Selvon, *Turn Again Tiger* (London: Heinemann, 1979), p.155. Subsequent references are cited in the text.

THE MALE MIND AND THE FEMALE HEART: SELVON'S WAYS TO KNOWLEDGE IN THE 'TIGER BOOKS'

PAOLA LORETO

> You will love these people, Foster.
> You will be amused that they are happy while you,
> equipped with so much that they haven't got,
> go on searching endlessly.
>
> Sam Selvon, *An Island Is a World*

The act of love is a microcosm mirroring the macrocosm of life. It is a symbolic gesture re-enacting the most significant experiences of our existence. The first sexual encounter between Tiger and Urmilla, the main characters of Sam Selvon's novel *A Brighter Sun* (1953), prefigures the steps they will make on their way towards maturity. The young couple have been forced into an early marriage by their parents' strict observance of traditional Indian habits. As their first night together is approaching, they think of the marital duty they have to perform with fear. They lack all instructions, and they feel they have to live up to each others' expectations, two conditions sufficient to make that duty more cumbersome than appealing.

They soon realise, though, that a powerful force dwells inside them which they will be able to 'switch on' simply by relaxing and being themselves.[1] They don't even know exactly what they are doing, Selvon writes, because it is the force – or 'power', or 'strength', as he calls it otherwise – that does everything. Their role in this act of discovery is to 'wonder at the new knowledge' they find the moment they stop anxiously hunting for it. The awakening of desire, which transcends their sense of duty, is what allows for this new awareness.

The same pattern of feelings and emotions recurs when Tiger and Urmilla behold the trees bearing fruit in their garden. Selvon's words are almost identical: 'Neither of them understood properly, but Tiger saw the wonder of it and grew to love the land more' (*A Brighter Sun*, 83). One important, new word does come in here, and that is love. Love is the form of knowledge that comes from an attitude of patient expectation and surrender to a powerful, superior force.

The male and the female characters in Selvon's novels reach this form of knowledge by different routes. The women's way seems to be the straighter one. It is walked demurely in silence. The men's way is more winding and sometimes seems to lose sight of its destination, but in the end it leads to the same place of happiness and freedom. The scenery is usually more impressive. A natural, vast landscape takes the place of a homely kitchen. But the feelings inside are the same and easily recognisable: it is when Tiger 'feels good' and 'free' that he 'smiles to himself'.

The novels in which Selvon is most concerned with the issue of his hero's growth are the so-called 'Tiger books', *A Brighter Sun* (1953) and its sequel, *Turn Again Tiger* (1958). These books deal with a young man's attempt at 'becoming a man' (or rather 'a big man', as he would have it) in a suburban village in Trinidad. Of East Indian origin, Tiger has to face a process of creolisation, that is, of integration into the multiracial and multicultural society of Barataria. In these books, as in all his other fiction set in Trinidad, Selvon focuses more on the female characters than in the 'London novels', where the West Indian community is almost uniquely made up by the men who first emigrated, alone, to England.

Contrary to the view expressed by Alessandra Dotti in her 1990 interview with Selvon, a strong case can be made that the characterisation of women in the Tiger books is as accomplished and powerful as that of the male figures.[2] The relationship between men and women, besides, is far more complex than how it has generally been described. Anson Gonzales, for example, claims that in Selvon's novels men relate to women exclusively as to the objects of their desire or the subjects of their will.[3] This harsh judgement can suit the part the female walk-ons play in the choral dimension of the Tiger books. It certainly fails to gather the rich essence of the central figures, Tiger and Urmilla. Husband and wife, man and woman, embody here two different and complementary ways of looking for wisdom and meaning in the individual's existence.

Tiger is the character Selvon mostly identifies with in his early fiction. There is also Moses, the hero of the London novels. Book after book, Selvon gets more and more involved in Moses's adventures, while his interest turns from the search for a personal maturity to the search for a writer's maturity. The Moses books are mainly a metanarrative of the writing of a book. It is with Tiger, therefore, that Selvon meditates on the adventure of growing up and at the same time tests with detachment his personal theory of knowledge.

Tiger is Selvon's point of departure, a character who gives voice to the author's drives: the restlessness he cannot get rid of, his urgent need for knowledge. The young man is obsessed with one, fundamental question: 'How long before he did the right thing, and said the right thing at the right time?'[4] He realises quite soon that becoming a man cannot mean to him what it means to many of the other men of Barataria: learning to smoke and drink and beat one's wife. He discovers that 'It take more than that' (*A Brighter Sun*, 109), and he sets out to hunt for a 'hidden understanding', fascinated by people who, like Tall Boy, seem to know 'a lot of answers' (*Turn Again Tiger*, 33).

As a figure, however, Tiger is never reduced to representing a single issue. The turns his psychological development takes, and the moves forwards and backwards in his path make him a thoroughly believable human being. Selvon is gifted in his ability to characterise with a single, well-aimed stroke. But his sketches do not result in stereotypes. His brush-strokes never flatten his volumes. On the contrary, they give his creations a plastic relief, that is, enough depth to reveal their humanity. It is often the observation of an attitude, or gesture, instead of a full description, that makes them vivid. It is Otto's comic, uncurable sleepiness, or More Lazy's intense and surreal dreaminess.

Tiger sets himself apart from the others by his own personal 'quirk', which is a compulsion to reason things out. While More Lazy, speaking in the incisive Trinidad Creole English, can say: 'I don't figure nothing out. I just is' (*Turn Again Tiger*, 100), for Tiger awareness is breath (*Turn Again Tiger*, 91). He may try and be satisfied with merely surviving, for a while, or with waiting for things to happen by themselves, as he sees his friends doing. But this will not last long. Sooner or later he will go back to feeling uncertain about everything, and hoping that knowledge – the final explanation of things, the source of all answers – 'would put him right' (*A Brighter Sun*, 76).

He begins by identifying knowledge with what one can read in books (*A Brighter Sun*, 78). But somehow this does not seem to work. When he asks one of the villagers, Sookdeo, how he manages to get good crops out of his garden without doing much work in it, the Indian answers that Tiger should not listen too carefully to the advice of the 'agriculture man from the government'. 'He have plenty book knowledge,' but 'Haveam some ting yuh learn only by experience.' What is still more important, experience teaches that the way of making the land fruitful is not to follow someone else's prescriptions, but 'to love de tings yuh plant' (*A Brighter Sun*, 77-78). And the earth seems to return Sookdeo's careless love for it (*A Brighter Sun*, p. 67).

This kind of instinctive knowledge normally belongs to the women of Barataria. It is true that also Joe, Tiger's black neighbour and friend, can tell him the secret of self-acceptance (*Turn Again Tiger*, 155), but Rita, Joe's wife, and Urmilla are grounded in an ancient, universal wisdom that allows them deep insights into life and into people's behaviours. Selvon's treatment of female figures is quite subtle. If properly understood, it is revealing of his intuition of a possible way to knowledge.

Of some of the female characters populating his fiction Selvon celebrates the sheer beauty, by which he seems to be fascinated himself. One particular kind of beauty appears to belong to Indian women like Urmilla in the short story 'Johnson and the Cascadura': 'Urmilla was the most beautiful Indian girl I had ever seen. It was a withdrawn sort of beauty, you only saw it when she was disturbed.'[5] This kind of description can take off for some lyrical flight such as this Shakespearean reminiscence: 'She looked up and where the eyes should have been I saw pearls' (*Ways of Sunlight*, 9).[6]

As he does in his male portraits, Selvon manages to stress the individuality of each woman through one single gesture, sometimes a real quirk. The indifference with which Berta possesses her natural beauty betrays the shyness that is deeply rooted under her apparent boldness: 'If she was unaware of a look or a glance she was beautiful, but once conscious of being looked at she twisted her body and frowned and grimaced and did all she could to appear ugly' (*Turn Again Tiger*, 67). In 'Cane is Bitter' Roomkin, 'frail but strong as most East Indian women', reveals a whole life of hard work and denial – in which desires and emotions have never been given a chance to live – by her habit of shutting her eyes when she is emotional, as if she knew the light she throws from them (*Ways of Sunlight*, 50).

Selvon's aesthetic perception of women – evidently helped by a personal, frank appreciation of them – provides him with thoughtful insights into the emotional development of human beings. The Urmilla of *A Brighter Sun* is first presented as 'having black, sad eyes, long hair, undeveloped breasts' (*A Brighter Sun*, 5). But through the experience of being a wife, and especially a mother, she develops a new consciousness which is directly reflected in her physical appearance:

> Shades of responsibility moved in her mind. From the time the baby had come, a new power had swept through her, like wind. She marvelled in it, moved her tongue in her mouth to see if she could taste the sweetness flowing through her. She moved her hands over her body and through her hair, and when she felt the baby at her side, she had thought, I is a woman now, and the thought had made her fearful and joyful at the same time. (*A Brighter Sun*, 48)

The passage is worth quoting because it is Selvon's best expression of the female way of coming to knowledge. Knowledge, for Urmilla, is not made of abstract deductions. It is not the fruit of hard thinking. Awareness comes to her through the sensations arising in her body from the metamorphosis of motherhood. That is why for her the sense of responsibility, that of a new power, and the taste of sweetness come together. The fear and joy she feels in her emotional coming of age show how the fulfilment of her being leads to an experience of wholeness of mind and body in which opposites are quietly and naturally reconciled.

The ability to experience such a feeling of blessedness distinguishes both Tiger and Urmilla from the other inhabitants of Barataria. The male and the female ways to knowledge are brought together and confronted in their relationship. Both of them have faith and hope in themselves, as if they were touched by grace. But being a man, Tiger has to look for such ecstatic moments in nature. It is in the fields that he is able to feel:

...the power... all around him... throbbing in the earth, humming in the air, riding the night wind, stealing through the swamp. The power was free: all you had to do was breathe it in, deep and full, until your chest felt like bursting. And glory in it – in the depth of the night, in the rustling trees, in the immense space between earth and sky. (*A Brighter Sun*, 113)

Tiger has to find a contact with earth and matter outside himself. This explains his problems in coping with reality. For Urmilla as for all the other women in the book, desire is satisfied by the apparently small achievements of everyday life, like a successful dinner. This is because what they desire is most of the time simply to be able to accomplish their duty, which in the best cases is a duty of love and giving. Even when it isn't reality, but fantasy to elicit a whim, this is nothing bigger than a new dress or a pair of high-heeled shoes.

Tiger, on the contrary, has higher ideals, that make acceptance of their imperfect fulfilment harder for him. He is often absorbed in the thought of God, while Urmilla focuses on his happiness: 'Whatever you do, I could only hope is for the best, and that it make you happy' (*Turn Again Tiger*, 93). He is constantly worried about what he should do or whether what he is doing is right. She is normally content with what he chooses to do.

If the ability to make choices is the most evident sign of a person's maturity, a lesser capacity for acceptance is what makes the act of choosing more difficult for Tiger. On the one hand it may appear that choices are easier to make for the women of Barataria: being less free to choose, they are more inclined to be contented with what they can achieve. On the other hand, a sort of resignation to the way life – and Selvon likes to stress, now and then, that it *is* a 'funny life' – is shared by their men. This, again, makes Tiger and Urmilla stand out from all the other villagers: Tiger for his greater expectations, Urmilla for her extraordinary refusal to passively submit to her husband's will when it shows to be unmistakably wrong.

Urmilla's attitude of acceptance is not indiscriminate. Even if she tries hard to please Tiger, she is not ready to give up some of her 'small' desires, like the possibility of enjoying her husband's company at the end of the day. Urmilla manages to take some part in the shaping of her married life when she becomes the leader of the women's rebellion against the men's habit of staying out drinking till late at night. Tiger is secretly proud of her, and this shows how the relationship between the two young people is one in which it is possible for a man and a woman to grow together.

Tiger and Urmilla let imagination come into their relationship so that they can find a new balance halfway between accepting reality and changing it.

Tiger approaches the choices he has to make in the same way he had approached his first sexual contact with Urmilla: as if it were a task, and afraid of the mistakes he could make in performing it. Afraid, that is, of not being able to live up to the idea of 'bigness' he has forged in his mind. In his initial childish expectations Tiger would have liked everything to be 'big'. Above all, he would have liked to become 'a big man'. But experience teaches him that 'Things happened. One thing led to another, and before you knew it there was a plan of action sketched out for you, and all you had to do was to follow it' (*Turn Again Tiger*, 11). This occurs to Tiger when he has to decide whether to accept his father's proposal to go and work with him as an overseer in a new sugar estate in the small village of Five Rivers. At first Tiger is frightened at the idea of what he might lose in choosing to go. But as soon as the choice has been made he feels a sense of great relief. That is precisely the way he makes his choices: he suddenly stops worrying about them, lets himself go in an act of surrender, and finally realises that the solution was already there, in the acceptance of the shape events are taking. Tiger doesn't need to *make* his choices: he *finds* them.

Urmilla, on her part, seems to know all this already. On the occasion of another choice Tiger has to make, he turns to his wife for advice, and asks her whether he should accept a humble job at the white overseer's house. Urmilla's answer is: 'I don't know, Tiger. I want to advise you if I could, but I don't know. Whatever you do, I could only hope for the best, and that it make you happy' (*Turn Again Tiger*, 93). Urmilla wishes for Tiger what she instinctively knows is good for her: that he could learn to surrender to an attitude of acceptance. That he could have faith and find in his heart that good feeling which alone can make life worth living.

Acceptance constantly exercised allows Urmilla to grow steadily, walking a linear path. The circles Tiger follows in his growth bring him to acceptance only now and then. They are wider and wider circles, though, which take in more and more of the harsh reality. An observation made at the end of the first book shows how his acknowledgement of the limits his social role imposes on him is still cautious and somewhat reluctant. When Boysie, who represents a feeling of freedom for Tiger, suggests that he sell

his house and go away to study to be a lawyer, the young father answers
that a man is not always able to do the things he wants to do (*A Brighter
Sun*, 213).

At the end of the second book, however, the reader can hear a more
convincing accent in Tiger's voice. Asked if he desires a boy-child, he answers: 'Whatever come, come. What is to is, must is' (*Turn Again Tiger*,
149). After the bitter disappointment at the birth of his first child, a daugh-
ter, this is a good step forward. At this point Tiger has become a free and
self-confident individual, who can take the consequences of his choices
upon himself without being subject to commonplace expectations.

The straight and keen perceptions of the women who make up his domestic entourage – Urmilla and her best friend, Rita – accurately register
his progress and its setbacks. There's no anger in Urmilla's words when
she quietly gets to the heart of the matter and tells Tiger that he only thinks
of himself (*Turn Again Tiger*, 126). As for Rita, the older woman is able to
appreciate Tiger's increasing maturity and at the same time to explain its
slowness: 'He's growing up like a real man now. Some things you can't
learn just like that. You have to wait until the good lord want you to know'
(*Turn Again Tiger*, 12).

Selvon's identification with the male heroes of his novels is always evident, but it becomes intentional in his 'straight' fiction, as he called it. To
this fiction belong the beautiful short story 'My Girl and the City',[7] *An
Island Is a World*,[8] and *I Hear Thunder* – the two novels dealing with the
existential and metaphysical crises of educated, middle-class heroes in-
habiting a post-war Trinidad. The tone in these works is completely different, certainly more confessional. Susheila Nasta rightly describes it as
introverted and reflective.[9] It is in Foster's words, in particular, in *An Island Is a World*, that we can hear the echo of Tiger's and Moses's words:

> After all the thought and the reasoning, the long nights with the world spin-
> ning in his brain, he had to make a choice. Why was it so difficult? Why
> couldn't one say yes or no and have done with all the complexity? Why
> hesitate and ponder, why weigh each thought, why spend life going round
> and round in circles, never getting there, always thinking, wondering what
> was the right thing to do? (*An Island Is a World*, 274-275)

The sequel to these painful, suffered reflections should also sound familiar, at this point: 'Perhaps life in the long run is only a reconciliation

to circumstances, made bearable by the thought that a freedom exists at hand always available' (*An Island Is a World*, 211).

When he gives voice to the female attitude towards the same issue, however, Selvon not only shows a deep knowledge of women's psychology, but a firm conviction of its soundness. In contrast to Foster's 'whys and wherefores', Jennifer offers her simple search for love and happiness. Not for the happiness which comes from being loved, but for that which comes from loving (*An Island Is a World*, 274). The fact that she is the woman who manages in the end – without much effort indeed – to make Foster think of marriage is revealing of the great power her way of loving has to affect the feelings and behaviour of the people around her.

The fruitfulness of a collaboration between man and woman in their search for a wise way of living is confirmed by the fact that marriage, on the whole, is a favourable institution in Selvon's fiction. In *The Housing Lark*, Fitz, despite the teasing he undergoes because of his submission to his resolute wife, in the end leads one of the most contented lives in the book.[10] And Harry, who is desperately in love, and, after marriage, shows clear signs of feeling happy inside. Life never loses its fresh meaning for him, not even when he is unjustly sent to jail. What is still more telling, Selvon treats the intimacy between husband and wife with a powerful mixture of humour and tenderness. The struggle between Otto, who runs the shop where the men gather to drink in the evening, and the women of Five Rivers, who want him to shut it earlier so that they can have their men at home with them, is won by the women thanks to his wife's cunning appeal: "'And listen" Berta went close and whispered in his ear, "when the men don't come to drink in the evening, you could shut the shop earlier, and you and me have more time together, eh?"' (*Turn Again Tiger*, 86).

Even Tiger's betrayal of Urmilla takes a legitimate place in his emotional development. On Tiger's part, this betrayal is even more apparent than real, because it can hardly be said to be an act of his will. It has little or nothing to do with love, and much more with an overwhelming passion that can deprive a man of his ability to choose. What should one do with this new and disrupting kind of feeling? There is a blind desire that turns out to be destructive, Tiger learns, and there is a desire that can work as the needle in a compass, revealing the heart's inclinations, orienting one's choices.

As far as he gives each of them equal credit, the male and female psychologies of knowledge, or ways of coping with existence and its harshness, are truly complementary in Selvon's fiction and, evidently, in his view. The only difference is a feeling of greater closeness to the male compared to a longing for the female, the kind of longing one has for what he is able to imagine, but cannot possess. In the Tiger books, the first feeling is the material Selvon derives from his personal experience and starts with, the second feeling is his attempt at working on that material with the tools of insight and imagination.

Selvon, though, is heading for no clear-cut theory of knowledge. He gives no ready-made answers for the restlessness in Tiger's heart. He brings Tiger close enough to the point of full maturity that he is able to accept death as the natural fulfilment of life (*A Brighter Sun*, 157). But right at this moment of acceptance Selvon makes his hero rebel at the idea that he should be content with 'just being, and maintaining an equilibrium in a place where nothing seemed worth living for', with sheer 'life, growing up, growing old, dying and rotting in six feet of earth' (*Turn Again Tiger*, 35). Through Sookdeo, Selvon teaches Tiger that one learns from experience rather than from books. But why, then, should he choose the same old man to inspire the young one and help him to read (*A Brighter Sun*, 155)?

The answer, perhaps, is in Selvon's own, personal choice to be a writer. And in the narrow rope he gives Tiger to walk on:

> There must be something fine and noble in everyday life, in the way you walked and talked, in the way you put on your shirt and ate breakfast in the morning. You had to give life reason and purpose, and try not to change it. (*Turn Again Tiger*, 111)

1 Sam Selvon, *A Brighter Sun* (New York: Viking Press, 1953), p.16. Further references will be given in the text.

2 It appears, though, that Dotti's opinion is widely shared. Selvon answers her question saying that 'Many people had said that I hadn't written very much about women in the book [*The Lonely Londoners*, 1956], but, I mean, that would be another novel... If I wanted, as a writer, if I planned to write a novel to show also the woman's point of view... I would have written a different kind of novel,' *Caribana*, 1 (1990), p.80. See also p.128 of this book.

3 Anson Gonzales, 'First of the Big Timers: Sam Selvon', in *Critical Perspectives on Sam Selvon*, ed. by Susheila Nasta (Washington, D.C.: Three Continents Press, 1988), pp.48-51.

4 Sam Selvon, *Turn Again Tiger* (London: Heinemann, 1979), p.6. Further references will be given in the text.

5 Sam Selvon, *Ways of Sunlight* (Harlow, Essex: Longman, 1987), p.6. Further references will be given in the text.

6 The line in Ariel's song in *The Tempest* goes 'Those are pearls that were his eyes' (I.ii.).

7 Selvon, *Ways of Sunlight*, pp.169-176.

8 Sam Selvon, *An Island Is a World* (London: Allan Wingate, 1955). Further references will be given in the text.

9 Susheila Nasta (ed.), *Critical Perspectives*, op. cit., p.5.

10 Sam Selvon, *The Housing Lark* (Washington, D.C.: Three Continents Press, 1990).

'THE WORLD TURN UPSIDE DOWN': CARNIVAL PATTERNS IN *THE LONELY LONDONERS*

JOHN THIEME

Summer does really be hearts like if you start to live again… oh it does really be beautiful then to hear the birds whistling and see the green leaves come back on the trees and in the night the world turn upside down and everybody hustling that is life that is London.[1]

Samuel Selvon, *The Lonely Londoners*

Carnival celebrated liberation from the prevailing truth and from the established order; it marked the suspension of all hierarchical rank, privileges, norms and prohibitions. Carnival was the true feast of time, the feast of becoming, change and renewal. It was hostile to all that was immortalised and completed.[2]

Mikhail Bakhtin, *Rabelais and His World*

The story of the East Indian experience in the Caribbean has by and large been one of acculturation, as the Hindu and Muslim social and religious codes, which the indentured labourers who came to work on the West Indian sugar plantations brought with them, have been eroded and metamorphosed in the creole melting pot. The process of creolisation has, however, been far from uniform and the work of V. S. Naipaul and Sam Selvon, the two most significant Caribbean East Indian writers to have emerged to date, illustrates very different responses to the attenuation of the cultures of the subcontinent. Arguably these responses emanate from the disparate upbringings of the two writers. Naipaul grew up in a fairly traditional

Brahminical family and in his early fiction writes almost exclusively about
the Indian community. Answering the charge that he fails to write about
the interaction between different racial groups, he says in *An Area of Darkness* (1964), the work which most fully explores his Indian origins:

> I have been rebuked by writers from the West Indies, and notably George
> Lamming, for not paying sufficient attention in my books to non-Indian
> groups. The confrontation of different communities, he said, was the fun-
> damental West Indian experience. So indeed it is, and increasingly. But to
> see the attenuation of the culture of my childhood as the result of a dra-
> matic confrontation of opposed worlds would be to distort the reality. To
> me the worlds were juxtaposed and mutually exclusive.[3]

In contrast, Selvon, who is a quarter Scottish, grew up in a hybrid milieu and is more concerned in his early fiction with East Indian assimilation. Though sometimes believed to be of peasant origins,[4] he describes
himself as a product of middle-class San Fernando, Trinidad's second city,
and makes the point that his upbringing was very different from that of
Tiger, the young East Indian protagonist of his novels *A Brighter Sun* (1952)
and *Turn Again Tiger* (1958).[5] In Naipaul's early novels Hindu beliefs and
practices are often mocked by a sardonic ironic voice, but one which nevertheless displays a degree of involvement with the rejected religion which
parallels that of the lapsed Catholic.[6] In Selvon's fiction the process of
acculturation has gone further and the authorial voice demonstrates none
of the obsessive intensity of feeling which characterises Naipaul's response
to the values of his ancestral culture.

In Selvon's first novels, which have Trinidadian settings, there are ves-
tigial traces of an attempt to explore a distinctively East Indian identity,
but once the location of his novels moves to England in *The Lonely Londoners* (1956) and the latter half of *Ways of Sunlight* (1957), such specifics
of identity are obscured. As in Naipaul's earliest work of fiction, *Miguel
Street* (1957), which in this respect is in marked contrast to his subsequent
work, the racial identity of most of the characters is indeterminate. In
Naipaul's case it is clear that a few of them, such as the boy narrator,
Bhakcu and Eddoes are East Indian, but the cultural codes to which the
bulk of the remainder subscribe – in particular an ethos inspired by the
calypso tradition and the Hollywood 'tough guy' – suggest initially that
they belong to the majority black population of Port of Spain. Consequently

it comes as something of a surprise to learn from Naipaul's recently published 'Prologue to an Autobiography' that characters like Hat and Bogart
are based on Indian real-life originals,[7] and, while it is at variance with
the dominant pattern of Naipaul's early fiction, which mainly portrays Indians as leading lives which insulate them from the community at large,
this provides further evidence of the extent of their assimilation.

In Selvon's case, almost paradoxically, since his own upbringing was
more creolised, the movement is in the opposite direction. It is only when
his fiction moves to *England* that the specifics of racial identity become
blurred in the way that they are in *Miguel Street*. In novels like *The Lonely
Londoners* the sense of racial and cultural identity is strong, but it is the
characters' awareness of themselves as West Indian or black more generally which provides this sense. Despite occasional passages which fore-
ground the differences between immigrants from various West Indian islands,[8] the text suggests that it is the move to England which has given
the characters a group identity as West Indians.

At the same time *The Lonely Londoners* represents an important formal advance in Selvon's fiction, as for the first time he writes in a distinctively West Indian narrative mode. His earlier novels had, apart from occasional passages which drew on the oral storytelling traditions of Trinidad,[9] been written in Standard English and within the conventions of
European social realist fiction. In contrast, *The Lonely Londoners* employs
a stylised form of Trinidad Creole as the medium of the fiction and
presents the narrative not as a continuous linear account, but as a series
of almost self-contained anecdotes, many of which have distinct affinities
with calypso, the dominant narrative genre of Trinidad. Writing about this
in 1982 I said:

> This adoption of a distinctively West Indian mode is a formal correlative
> of the themes of the novel: Selvon is dramatising the conflict between West
> Indian value-systems and those of the English 'host culture' and in so do-
> ing does, I would argue, subvert the norms of the novel genre. As for his
> Indianness, this is totally forgotten, to a point where it is almost impossi-
> ble to determine which of his lonely Londoners are of Indian descent. In
> the Trinidad novels he writes as an Indian, albeit a Creolised one; in the
> 'English' novels, he writes as a West Indian.[10]

If anything, this fails to do justice to the nature and extent of Selvon's
innovation in *The Lonely Londoners*. The novel is in every sense – form

and theme become inextricable – an embodiment of Trinidadian carnivalesque values.

For the Russian formalist critic Mikhail Bakhtin, European carnival represents an alternative mode of discourse to those of the dominant Establishment culture, whether it be that of the Catholic church or the rationalist society of the post-Renaissance era. For Bakhtin carnival is parodic, egalitarian and subversive. He says of carnivals and related marketplace festivals: 'They were the second life of the people, who for a time entered the utopian realm of community, freedom, equality and abundance.'[11] The parallels with Trinidadian Carnival, which first evolved into something like its present form in the nineteenth century, when emancipated slaves and their descendants appropriated and subverted the fêtes of the European plantocracy,[12] are fairly precise. Trinidad Carnival takes place at the same time of year, in the pre-Lenten period, and affords very similar opportunities for inversion, parody and renewal.[13] In its use of parody, it has much in common with traditional carnivalesque parody, which, in Bakhtin's view,[14] is antithetical to modern formal parody in that it revives and renews at the same time as it denies. Bakhtin is mainly interested in carnival as a system of discourse and he makes the further point that in certain major European writers who take issue with the dominant literary conventions of their day – Rabelais, Cervantes, Shakespeare and Dostoevsky are among them – a process of carnivalisation of form occurs, as they bring the neglected oral idioms of the folk culture, the culture of carnival and the marketplace, into the world of the printed book. So, on this level, carnivalisation is what happens when the oral tradition invades the domain of literature.

It takes little imagination to see the possible implications of this theory for West Indian culture, where the attempt at emancipation from an imposed European system of values in the late colonial period and the post-Independence era has produced a creative tension between the inherited literary tradition and the oral tradition, with the latter increasingly asserting its presence in writing and bringing about a reassessment of whether written literature (as traditionally conceived) should continue to be a privileged discourse. Poets such as Louise Bennett, Edward Brathwaite and, more recently, Michael Smith, Linton Kwesi Johnson and the dub poets have stressed the importance of performance; dramatists such as Derek Walcott and Errol Hill have introduced carnival elements into the theatre of the region; and novelists like V. S. Reid, George Lamming and Earl Lovelace have creolised the form of the novel by placing oral storytelling elements at the heart of their fictions.

Selvon's works occupy a central position among West Indian carnival texts and none more so than *The Lonely Londoners*. Though it was not the first novel to employ a form of Caribbean Creole as the narrative voice – this honour belongs to Reid's *New Day* (1949) – and though it is set in England and does not include any episodes from an actual carnival, *The Lonely Londoners* may reasonably be viewed as the seminal West Indian carnival text, since it combines an oral narrative voice with the parodic, egalitarian and subversive comedy of Bakhtinian carnival. The use of such a narrative voice collapses the distance between the literary tradition and the oral culture of the protagonists.

Consider the difference between these two versions of a common story: the first is taken from *Miguel Street*, the second from *The Lonely Londoners*:

> What happened afterwards wasn't really unexpected.
> Man-man announced that he was a new Messiah.
> Hat said one day, 'You ain't hear the latest?'
> We said, 'What?'
> 'Is about Man-man. He say he going to be crucified one of these days.'
> 'Nobody go touch him,' Edward said. 'Everybody fraid of him now.'
> Hat explained. 'No, it ain't that. He going to crucify hisself. One of these Fridays he going to Blue Basin and tie hisself to a cross and let people stone him.'
> We walked to Blue Basin, the waterfall in the mountains to the north-west of Port of Spain, and we got there in two hours. Man-man began carrying the cross from the road, up the rocky path and then down to the Basin.
> Some men put up the cross, and tied Man-man to it.
> Man-man said, 'Stone me, brethren.'
> The women wept and flung bits of sand and gravel at his feet.
> Man-man groaned and said, 'Father, forgive them. They ain't know what they doing.' Then he screamed out, 'Stone me, brethren!'
> A pebble the size of an egg struck him on the chest.
> Man-man cried, 'Stone, stone, STONE me brethren! I forgive you.'
> Edward said, 'The man really brave.'
> People began flinging really big stones at Man-man, aiming at his face and chest.
> Man-man looked hurt and surprised. He shouted, 'What the hell is this? What the hell you people think you doing? Look, get me down from this thing quick, and I go settle with that son of a bitch who pelt a stone at me.'

From where Edward and Hat and the rest of us stood, it sounded like a cry of agony.

A bigger stone struck Man-man; the women flung the sand and gravel at him.

We heard Man-man's shout, clear and loud, 'Cut this stupidness out. Cut it out, I tell you. I finish with this arseness, you hear.' And then he began cursing so loudly and coarsely that the people stopped in surprise.

The police took away Man-man.

The authorities kept him for observation. Then for good.[15]

Moses laugh. 'You hear bout the time they nail Brackley to the cross?' he ask Galahad.

'No.'

'One Sunday morning they nail Brackley to the cross up on Calvary Hill. You know where that is? Up there behind the Dry River, as you going up Laventille. Well it had a gang of wayside preachers, and Brackley join them, and he decide this morning to make things look real. So he tell them to nail him to the cross before they start to preach. Brackley stretch out there, and they drive nails between his fingers and tie up his hands with twine. Brackley look as if he really suffering. A test went and get a bucket of cattle blood and throw it over him, and Brackley hang up there while the way-side preachers start to preach. The leader take out a white sheet and spread it on the ground, and three-four women stand up with hymnbook in their hand, and they singing and preaching. But them boys start to make rab. They begin with little pebbles, but they gradually increase to some big brick. Brick flying all by Brackley head until he start to bawl, "Take me down from here!" Brackley shout. "They didn't stone Christ on the cross!" And this time big macadam and rock flying all about in the air.'

Galahad laugh until tears come, and Moses suddenly sober up, as if it not right that in these hard times he and Galahad could sit there, belly full with pigeon, smoking cigarette, and talking bout them characters back home. (112)

The tale is a popular folk story, which has been celebrated in calypso.[16] So initially it might seem that both texts incorporate a carnivalesque narrative from the oral tradition. However, closer examination reveals a considerable difference in the way in which this has happened. In *Miguel Street* the story is retold by the young boy narrator as part of his account of Man-man's history; in *The Lonely Londoners* Moses, the central character, re-tells it in direct speech as an incidental anecdote. Both versions exploit the comic potential of the story and both versions use creole, but in

Naipaul's case dialect is reserved for the dialogue, while in Selvon's the whole story is circumscribed within the inverted commas which denote Moses's voice and when it is over, there is no appreciable change of register as the third-person narrator resumes the narrative. In *Miguel Street* dialect is partly used for the purpose of satirical diminution of character (a standard device of pre-twentieth-century colonial fiction), as Man-man, who has previously been described as speaking with 'a correct and very English accent',[17] breaks down into creole. So here the change in register is an index of the character's inability to sustain an assumed role – not simply that of Christ, but more generally that of someone who is superior by virtue of his having crossed the linguistic divide between coloniser and colonised. In *The Lonely Londoners* the comedy is altogether more compassionate, as Moses and Galahad share the fun of 'them boys… mak[ing] rab' without distancing themselves from or diminishing Brackley. In both passages the comedy gives way to a more sombre tone in the denouement, but here too there is a considerable difference. Man-man's story concludes with the boy's Standard English authorial voice maintaining distance from the events he describes, as is the case at every point in the text, and the effect of this is to establish an ambience in which the voice of an assessing ironist mediates between the narrative and the readership. It is a mode of presentation which has much in common with the English ironic tradition. In contrast, once the account of Brackley's 'crucifixion' is completed, the narrative voice continues to speak in essentially the same idiom. The change in tone which we also get here arises not from an implied dismissal of the values embodied in the story – indeed such 'oldtalk' seems to provide sustenance amid the 'hard times' of living in London – but rather because Moses pulls himself up for indulging in such pleasant nostalgia. So *The Lonely Londoners* is carnivalesque in a way that *Miguel Street*, for all its use of calypso themes and allusions, is not: the distance between the oral and the literary has been totally collapsed.

The lack of any significant distinction between the idiom in which the characters speak and the language of the authorial voice has led some readers to feel that the third-person narrator can be identified with Moses. Such a view is lent credence by the fact that he is the centre of consciousness in passages like the one quoted above. Moreover, the way the authorial voice moves between celebrating the joys of London life and feeling alienated and displaced in the metropolis parallels a similar alternation in Moses's

moods, which appears as the product of a more reflective consciousness
than that of most of the characters. So Moses seems to be close to the author figure and this is particularly apparent in the closing sentences of the
novel, where there is a suggestion that perhaps he is a writer in the making:

> Daniel was telling him how over in France all kinds of fellars writing
> books what turning out to be best-sellers. Taxi-driver, porter, road-sweeper
> – it didn't matter. One day you sweating in the factory and the next day all
> the newspapers have your name and photo, saying how you are a new lit-
> erary giant.
>   He watch a tugboat on the Thames, wondering if he could ever write a
> book like that, what everybody would buy. (126)

Nevertheless it is difficult to sustain the view that the authorial voice
is, to all intents and purposes, Moses's, not only because he is not dramatised as such, but also because there are whole episodes of the text in which
he disappears and in these sections there is a similar breakdown of distance between the language of the authorial voice and that of *other* characters. When Big City is first introduced, a few swift brush strokes caricature him, in a manner typical of the novel's comic mode of character construction, through his language errors:

> Big City come from an orphanage in one of the country district in Trini-
> dad. When he was a little fellar, he hear some people talking about the
> music the norphanage band does play. But instead of hearing 'music' Big
> City thought he hear 'fusic' and since that time nobody could ever get him
> to say music. (77-78)

What is striking about this passage is the way the authorial voice makes a
similar kind of language error to that which it is attributing to Big City in
referring to 'the *n*orphanage', after having successfully rendered 'orphanage' when first referring to it. Again, it is an index of the equation of character and narrative voice, but in this instance the specific nature of the
characterisation – a form of caricature really – means that the author has
taken on a quite different identity and a quite different idiom from Moses's. So the authorial voice emerges as chameleon-like, as it assumes the
hue of whatever character it is talking about at the time. After Galahad
and Big City have enthused about the delights of London life, the narrator engages in a similar rhapsody. When Moses and Galahad indulge in

'oldtalk', the narrator becomes similarly nostalgic. Perhaps most promi-
nently of all, when the mood changes with the coming of summer and the
'boys' – the young, single males, who, with the single exception of the figure of Tanty, an older Jamaican woman, make up the novel's portrait gallery of main characters – are filled with a sense of seasonal and sexual
renewal, it is the narrator who becomes their spokesman. He does this in
a passage of eight pages of unpunctuated, lyrical prose, the 'summer is
hearts' passage, in which the form seems to have been totally carnivalised
as a Bakhtinian 'feast of becoming, change and renewal' runs riot with
the normal dictates of syntax. The style employed here is not, however, a
departure from that used elsewhere in the novel, only an intensification
of the oral, episodic method of the whole work.

Oral storytelling lies at the heart of the novel's structure and perhaps
provides the clearest indication of the extent to which the narrator may be
viewed as 'one of the boys', since the series of episodic tales which together
form his narrative is akin to a collection of the stories the boys tell one
another. If at first these seem like so many short stories of the same kind
as those which appear in *Ways of Sunlight*, ultimately their very random-
ness begins to shape itself into a pattern, as becomes clear in the closing
pages, where the repetition of key phrases from the characters' conversations points toward the repetitiveness and essentially centrifugal nature of
their lives:

> Hello boy, what happening.
>   So what happening, man, what happening.
>   How long you in Brit'n boy?
>   You think this winter bad? You should of been here in 52.
>   What happening, what happening man.
>   What the arse happening, lord? What all of us doing, coasting lime,
> Galahad asking if anybody know the words of the song Maybe It's Because
> I'm A Londoner, Cap wants two pounds borrow, Five only in town for
> the night and he want to know if he could sleep in Moses room, Big City
> coming tomorrow to full up the coupons (I nearly hit them last week),
> Lewis saying that Agnes come begging and if he should go to live with her
> again, Tolroy want to send Ma and Tanty back to Jamaica (them two old
> bitches, I don't know why they don't dead). (124)

and suggests that the characters are caught in a kind of cyclic determinism which prevents them from achieving meaningful self-fulfilment:

> Under the kiff-kiff laughter, behind the ballad and the episode, the what-happening, the summer-is-hearts, [Moses] could see a great aimlessness, a great restless, swaying movement that leaving you standing in the same spot. As if a forlorn shadow of doom fall on all the spades in the country. (125)

So the novel ends on a more sombre note, questioning the ability of the lonely Londoners' carnival lifestyle to adequately sustain them. If, on the one hand, it represents a healthy subversion of the essentially alien English value system, on the other hand, it also becomes a form of self-evasion.

A similar debate has flourished in Trinidad for many years, with some commentators arguing that carnival provides an important and much needed release and others arguing that it has produced an escapist mentality which has become the dominant character trait of the Trinidadian mentality and which has stood in the way of social progress.

In Selvon's London context, however, the question becomes particularly problematic, since his West Indian characters find themselves in a society which is traditionally antipathetic to the carnival mentality and so there is a particularly acute level of cultural conflict. On numerous occasions some form of creolisation of their English milieu seems to provide the characters with the ability to survive amid the alienating fog which, from the opening paragraph of the novel, is the dominant image of London life, making the city seem 'unreal' and like 'some strange place on another planet' (7). Tanty persuades her local grocer to 'trust' (63), to extend credit until the end of the week, a practice which he has always firmly resisted in the past. Galahad remembers his father catching pigeons for food in San Fernando and begins snatching them in Kensington Gardens, thereby incurring the wrath of an English animal lover. In both cases the conflict may be seen as involving a clash between a pragmatic marketplace culture and a more rigidly ordered system of rules and prohibitions. So here too one may speak of a carnivalisation of experience taking place.

Such a process is most evident in an episode which occurs toward the end of the novel, the dance organised by the anglophile Harris, who is the epitome of the assimilated immigrant, a would-be black Englishman:

> Harris is a fellar who like to play ladeda, and he like English customs and thing, he does be polite and say thank you and he does get up in the bus and the tube to let woman sit down, which is a thing even them

Englishmen don't do. And when he dress, you think it some Englishman going to work in the city, bowler and umbrella, and briefcase tuck under the arm, with *The Times* fold up in the pocket so the name would show, and he walking upright like if is he alone who alive in the world. Only thing, Harris face black. (95)

In contrast, Five Past Twelve, one of the 'boys' who attends the dance, is the epitome of the carnival mentality; he is a subversive, weed-smoking, womanising picaroon, eternally questing for 'fetes':

Five have woman all over London, and no sooner he hit the big city than he fly round by Moses to find out what happening, which part have fete and so on. For Five like a fete too bad. The time when the Lord Mayor did driving through London, it had a steel band beating pan all in the Circus, and you should know Five was in the front, jumping up as if a West Indian carnival. (94-95)

Five's carnivalesque response to the Lord Mayor's Show, a ceremony which symbolises civic propriety, prefigures his behaviour at Harris's dance. Although it is an essentially West Indian occasion with a steel band playing, the besuited Harris posts himself on the door and warns the boys not to 'make rab and turn the dance into a brawl' (96). They all pose a threat, but none more so than Five. When he arrives, Harris asks him not to misbehave and he replies by reminding him 'You forget I know you from back home. Is only since you hit Brit'n that you getting on so English' (97). Shortly afterwards Tanty further cuts Harris down to size by recalling the days when he used 'to run about the barrack-yard in shirt-tail!' (98). In what follows, a carnival atmosphere clearly takes over. All the characters who have hitherto been the subjects of individual episodes now come together in a communal breaking down of structures. The 'bacchanal' atmosphere of Port of Spain has been transferred to London and Harris finds that 'a real carnival slackness' (99) subverts the orderly social occasion he has planned. Only he and his English guests refrain from dancing initially, but not for long. Tanty grabs Harris and forces him to dance with her to the strains of her favourite calypso, 'Fan Me Saga Boy Fan Me'.[18] So, as in so much carnival comedy, there is a parodic inversion of roles as the pompous and self-important Harris is cast by Tanty in the role of the saga boy, the womanising 'glamour boy' of Trinidadian society from the 1940s onward,[19] a figure much celebrated in calypso. The full irony of this becomes apparent when one realises that the saga boy persona has, in effect, been adopted by the bulk of the other characters, particularly Five, but not Harris.

While Tanty dances with Harris, Five, already high, and Big City begin dancing with the white women Harris has invited and as the pace of the dance becomes increasingly frenetic, a complete carnivalisation of experience seems to have occurred. The section ends with Harris trying to persuade the boys to stand still during the playing of the National Anthem, a doomed attempt to impose stasis on the kinetic, antiauthoritarian spirit which has taken over the dance.

This episode may, then, be regarded as the central carnival experience of the novel, as both in form and theme it marks, again in Bakhtin's terminology, 'the suspension of all hierarchical rank, privileges, norms and prohibitions'. It is, however, not without ambiguity in its presentation of carnival values. While the dance is going on, Moses hovers ambivalently on the sidelines, his attitude poised somewhere between those represented by Harris and Five. Asked by Galahad whether he 'ever hit a weed' (104), he claims he has. Similarly, he tells Five, who says he has not seen him dancing, that he has had one or two dances. But this does not obscure the fact that his role is largely spectatorial and suggests a perspective which, while it is in no sense hostile to the generally bacchanalian atmosphere of the occasion, retains a certain degree of detachment from it. And the centrality of Moses in other sections of the narrative makes his viewpoint one which attracts a fair degree of reader sympathy.

In conclusion, *The Lonely Londoners* is a seminal carnival text in that it subverts the norms of the dominant tradition of Western fiction by instating the oral in the place of the literary; and many of the incidents described involve a parallel creolisation of experience. Yet the novel stops short of simply celebrating carnival values. While they seem to provide the characters with a *modus vivendi*, ultimately it is questionable whether this is not a form of self-evasion, for the boys' lifestyle is based on 'oldtalk' and there is little sense of a new culture being created or carnival values metamorphosed to enable them to deal with life in England.

Returning to the questions raised about the carnival mentality in Trinidad, one may argue that so long as carnival is a genuine expression of the culture of the marketplace, it provides through parody, subversion and irony a source of renewal, but once it becomes commercialised and co-opted as an arm of the Establishment, this potential disappears to be replaced all too easily by facile escapism. A further sea change occurs with the transplantation of the carnival ethos to the metropolis. Now it needs to accommodate the everyday reality of the new social situation. *The Lonely Londoners* suggests that in the English environment it continues to provide sustenance up to a point and that it is certainly a preferable lifestyle to any afforded by the host culture, but, as is made clear in the final pages, it is not finally adequate. The characters' continual repetitions of patterns of behaviour and discourse which rely on nostalgia suggest that the carnivalesque has become ossified and is ceasing to function as a force for 'becoming, change and renewal'.

---

1 Sam Selvon, *The Lonely Londoners* (London: Alan Wingate, 1956 and Longman, 1972), pp.90 and 93. Subsequent references are to the Longman edition and are cited in the text.

2 Mikhail Bakhtin, *Rabelais and His World*, trans. by Helene Iswolsky (Cambridge, Mass. and London: M.I.T. Press, 1965), p.10.

3 V. S. Naipaul, *An Area of Darkness* (London: André Deutsch, 1964; Harmondsworth: Penguin, 1970), p.35.

4 See, for example, George Lamming, *The Pleasures of Exile* (London: Michael Joseph, 1960), p.45.

5 'Oldtalk', Sam Selvon interviewed by John Thieme, *Caribana*, 1 (1990), pp.72-73. See also p.118 of this book.

6 See my article 'V. S. Naipaul and the Hindu Killer', *Journal of Indian Writing in English*, (July 1981), pp.70-86.

7 See particularly *Finding the Centre: Two Narratives* (London: André Deutsch, 1984), pp.18-19: 'Hat was our neighbour on the street. He wasn't negro or mulatto. But we thought of him as half-way there. He was a Port of Spain Indian... we thought of the other Indians in the street only as street people.'

8 See, for example, pp.10 and 113.

9 See, for example, the openings of several of the chapters of *A Brighter Sun*, where Selvon includes brief anecdotal accounts of local Trinidad 'characters'.

10 John Thieme, 'Rama in Exile: The Indian Writer Overseas', in *The Eye of the Beholder: Indian Writing in English*, ed. by Maggie Butcher (London: The Commonwealth Institute, 1983), p.72.

11 Bakhtin, p.9.

12 See Errol Hill, *The Trinidad Carnival: Mandate for a National Theatre* (Austin and London: University of Texas Press, 1972), chapter 2.

13 *Pace* the view which sees it as essentially escapist and/or commercial, though clearly both these dimensions are present in contemporary carnival.

14 Bakhtin, p.10.

15 V. S. Naipaul, *Miguel Street* (London: André Deutsch, 1959; Harmondsworth: Penguin, 1971), pp.42-44.

16 In the third stanza of The Mighty Wonder's 'Follow Me Children', quoted by Landeg White, *V. S. Naipaul: A Critical Introduction* (London: Macmillan, 1975), p.50.

17 V. S. Naipaul, *Miguel Street*, Penguin edition, p.39.

18 A recording of this calypso is available on *Calypso Cavalcade*, vol. III, Request Records, no.SLP745.

19 On the saga boy figure, see Keith Warner, *The Trinidad Calypso* (London: Heinemann, 1983), pp.98ff. and Gordon Rohlehr, 'Sparrow as Poet', in *David Frost Introduces Trinidad and Tobago* (London: André Deutsch, 1975), pp.85ff.

SAMUEL SELVON'S LINGUISTIC EXTRAVAGANZA:
MOSES ASCENDING

MAUREEN WARNER-LEWIS

Errol Hill's suggested paradigm of Trinidad Carnival, as a model for both moulding and interpreting the Trinidad theatre, is particularly apt for appreciating certain distinguishing artistic features of Samuel Selvon's oeuvre.[1] The episodic narrative structure of *The Lonely Londoners* can be related to the calypso format;[2] yet even in the context of a firmly contoured story-line in *Moses Ascending*, Selvon still resorts to another calypso technique – that of the final, humorously ironic twist characteristic of the anecdotal kaiso. But one can also interpret the loose thematic juxtaposition of episodes in Selvon's work as reflecting the disconnected thematic units called 'bands' which together cohere to form the macrocosmic festival, Carnival. Furthermore, Selvon may be said to have recaptured the exuberance and eclecticism of the Carnival pageant in the linguistic manipulation exhibited in *Moses Ascending*. Besides, the sheer verbal virtuosity of *Moses Ascending* itself recalls the extravaganza of a 'pretty mas' – a costume not merely representing a thematic motif, but 'o'er picturing' reality by imaginative and decorative excesses, a flattering parody.

Moses Ascending updates the situation and fortunes of the West Indian immigrant population in England. Its setting is the 1970s – the Black Power era – whereas *The Lonely Londoners* (1956), some stories in *Ways of Sunlight* (1957), and *The Housing Lark* (1965) had chronicled in fiction the immigrant conditions of the previous decade. The predominantly omniscient narrative voice of these sequences had emphasised the cultural and psychological comfort afforded the economic exiles by the 'old talk' of ballad reminiscence, by 'mamaguy', and 'picong'.[3] By the 1970s, however, the West Indian immigrant, epitomised by Moses, had become acculturated to a British lifestyle. The daydreams of physical return to roots had largely evaporated. Selvon recreates this shift of perspective. Having recourse to a thematic tradition in West Indian literature – the acquisition of shelter[4] – the parameters of Moses's ambition extend now to landlordship, and the accumulation of wealth at the expense of the new generation of Black British, both Caribbean and Asian. As such, this socialised immigrant culture reproduces its own parallel British caste/class system: Selvon's chief character, Moses, aspires to gentility. Himself an economic commodity in British imperial commerce, he has come to an understanding of the economic foundations of the gentry, that is, manipulation of the commodity markets – whether human or inorganic. He is also well aware that in the Old World artistic sensitivity is considered a necessary refinement of the nobility. So now a landlord – or rather, in his perceptions, a lord of the manor and therefore a man of leisure – Moses cultivates and displays his 'immortal longings' by committing his 'memoirs' to paper.[5]

This theme of cultural assimilation is fashioned by Selvon's humorous and ironic vision into a parody of the symbiotic relationship between the migrant and his host culture, indeed between West Indian and European cultures, and at a wider level, between the Third World and the developed metropole. Selvon caps his satiric intent by co-opting the first person narrative technique. Comedy – and there's plenty of it – is now not directed at the immigrant/victim by the confident narrator or balladeer; instead, the authoritative cosmopolitan man-of-affairs and experience will tell his own story. And his language will reflect the perils of any acculturation process through its bizarre juxtapositions and comic excesses, through Moses's synthesis of popular and formal cultures, and of his semi-literacy and book-learning. This linguistic hybridisation and extravaganza will betray and underscore the marginal status of the migrant, the outsider, the fluctuations attendant on his tenuous social and economic position, and the psychological confusions bred by his internalised upward class mobility.

The ironic metaphor of rise and decline which Selvon manipulates on a situational level is masterfully paralleled on the linguistic plane, for *Moses Ascending* presents an indulgent satire of the language of the social alien, the 'hurry-come-up', the 'johnny-come-lately', the *arriviste*.

Selvon achieves this satiric effect by the swiftness of transition in language register,[6] itself dependent on context:

TEXT	USAGE LEVEL
...I had forsaken my friends, and	Formal
...there was no more	
pigfoot and peas and rice,	Intimate, West Indian
nor even a cuppa	Intimate, English slang
to be obtained, even if they came	Formal, Sacred Biblical
with gifts of myrrh and frankincense.[7]	

Some of these are idiomatic in source and reflect the balance and parallelism, or the alliteration and assonance characteristic of that format. The abundance of clichés in the stylistic repertoire of Moses stamps him as 'the ordinary man', the 'man in the street', the undistinguished 'man of the people', who speaks in the ready-made catch phrases of the native language exponent.

Slang expressions produce the same effect:

I got him cracking (10)
came back pissed (11)

The Black Power cultural and political context of the action in the novel justifies the occurrence of the Afro-American 'cool' (17), 'way out' (17) and 'rags' (16).

Another stylistic form which produces a familiarity of tone is that of limerick-type rhyme – a technique intrinsic to poetry, whether from Africa or England – and harnessed by the now near-extinct *pierrot grenade* masquerader of Trinidad, as well as by the present-day Jamaican dub singer, d.j., and poet:

a man for all seasons and reasons (51)
the more liable, and pliable (27)
I could feel my inspiration draining away like perspiration (54)

Phrases snatched from popular music also fulfil the function of cultivating easy rapport with his audience. The range extends from the calypso 'Last Train to San Fernando' of the 1940s to the Mighty Sparrow's 'Drunk and Disorderly' of the 1970s. And Sparrow's pillage of the Bible for the perversely applied metaphor in 'Jean and Dinah' finds a parallel here in 'I earned my piece of cunt by the sweat of my brow' (107). Moses also modifies a favourite Christmas carol in 'of a cold winter's morn' (13). He further utilises the lyrics of popular tunes like 'Cat on a Hot Tin Roof', 'Happy Days Are Here Again', 'Que Será, Será', and vulgarises the 'To Arms' chorus of the 'Marseillaise'.

Similarly, the use of Trinidad English idioms captures with verisimilitude a casual speaking voice:

> if I lie I die (88)
> mad to bust a cane in my arse (37)
> every manjack (54)
> he could well see (68)
> my blood take him (10)
> every Friday please God (10)
> make rab (i.e., 'behave in a disorderly fashion') (81)
> it have a heaven which part (i.e., 'there's a heaven where') (20)

Trinidadian proverbial expressions also convey the tenor of a speaker rooted in the verbal lore and philosophic mainstays of his culture:

> monkey smoke your pipe (74)
> when you crooked you bend (73)
> after we is weevil (41)

The same effect is achieved by his recourse to the words of a school game: 'I spy with my little eye' (42).

Basilectal[8] Trinidad English is also evidenced in grammatical usage: the lack of subject-verb concord:

> men was fighting (42)
> as the dogs is so well trained (55)

the formal non-differentiation of past and present tenses:

> he was ... roaming through bedsitter land, picking out secondhand miscellany he need (7)

the invariant singular for plural noun designation:

> woman thumping out left and right with kick and cuff (43)

the indiscriminate occurrence of 'her' and 'she' as verb complement (see below) as well as double negation:

> he would not of bought no end-of-terrace house (7)

and reliance on onomatopoeia for dramatic aural effect:

> bragadam, biff (76).

The real-life situation of diglossia which obtains in the language performance of the majority of Trinidadians[9] is reflected in the fact that Moses does not stick rigidly to basilectal Trinidad English grammatical structures, but varies them with Standard English even in semantically identical phrases, such as:

> Bob pounce on she ... he just grab hold of her and start to drag she to the
> sofa (29)
> woman was screaming, men was just thumping out left and right (43)

In addition, mesolectal[10] hypercorrection surfaces in constructions like,

> the latters (103)
> she must of realised (26)
> But I didn't know nothing about sheeps (56)

The foregoing techniques are crucial in establishing for Moses a con-
fidential tone. But the I-narrator takes himself far too seriously to be content with this familiar, casual, and – no doubt to his way of thinking –
vulgar style. As a self-made man literally on the way up, and as a rather
self-conscious artist, Moses can manipulate a formal matter-of-fact contemporary Standard English register:

> It was Sir Galahad who drew my attention to the property (7)

or the more affectively heightened register imparted by syntactic inversion:

> Little did he dream (7)

He can speak too in the register of the business executive or bureaucrat:

> I want a complete dossier on these Pakis ... and furthermore you had bet-
> ter start keeping an inventory of our stock. (40-41)

Moses is also *au courant* with erudite worlds like 'insubordinate', 'per-
ambulate', 'nefarious', 'conundrum', and 'decimalise', and can spice his
language with non-English words and phrases: from the French –
bonhomie, in lieu; Latin – *bona fide, trivia, flagrento delicto* [sic]; German
– *spiel*. Scots English provides 'bonny',[11] and 'wee tot'.

But Selvon's artistic purpose is to frustrate any sustained gravity of tone,
and so, Moses falls into the errors of malapropism:

> coop de grace (62)
> peddle my own canoe[12] (46)
> parabox (68)
> writing my Memoirs in retrospective (45)
> lions (for 'loins') (71)
> to ditto (71)

Linked to malapropisms is the pretentiousness of his bombastic phrasing. In 'a battery of chunky signet rings, wearing them on unconventional digits' (17), Moses's hyperbolic synonym for 'fingers' helps to achieve a snooty distance from the vulgarity of the ring-wearer. In the following, an ill-founded snobbery emanates not only from the obvious semantic content of the phrase, but is underscored by the hypercorrect choices of the vague but analysis-bound lexeme 'aspects' in 'the respectable aspects of the meeting' (104).

   While Moses's linguistic uncertainty in 'received'[13] and literary English dialectia leads him into malapropisms, his self-perception as a writer affords him license to create neologisms:

> myrading chandeliers (12)
> hither-and-thithering (27)
> quasi-frontage (50)

He can also coin original images. Unfortunately for Moses's self-image, however, but fortunately for the ebullient humour of the novel, Moses does not always achieve a thematic synchronisation of image and objective context. Bob, the Northern Englishman, is described as standing up after a blow 'swaying like a coconut tree on the beach in a strong wind' (30), and Brenda, the black British girl after whom he lusted, is depicted as disgustedly flinging her maxi skirt across the room 'like one of them Mayaro fishermen casting his net' (31).[14] More appropriate, by reason of its reverse colonial resonances,[15] is Moses's account of how he had Bob 'toting armchair and dumbwaiter on his back like a safari porter' (40). Another brilliant simile is achieved when Moses co-opts the balletic carnival figures of the bat-cum-imp from the 'Devil band' and at the same time exploits the polysemy of 'wings' – alluding at once to the bat costume's wide wings and to stage wings:

> I leap on the platform like a bat out of hell hoping to make an escape in the wings. (103)

And his description of himself 'panting and breathing like a blacksmith bellows' (107) captures the heat and violence of the action.

But Moses continues to trip over his literary embellishments when he indulges in semantic redundancies of the type:

> I was never so happy to see somebody in my life before (44)
> I begin to think that suppose (36)

But his rhetorical flights achieve a versatility of tone: that of heightened drama:

> I was helplessly and hopelessly entangled and ensnared (78)
> I mulled, I mooned, I went into a brown study (52)

or the anti-climatic:

> I try the lock; it lock. (40)

They also confirm his potential for pun and oxymoron:

> to augment the argument (14)
> He maintain a vocal silence (46)

The overall dissonance of language register functions then as a thematic device as well as a formal means of character delineation. In tandem with this carefully orchestrated technique, Selvon intensifies the burlesque tenor of his work by a wide – one might say, bewildering and Eliotesque – range of literary allusions and echoes.[16] By investing the socially and linguistically mercurial Moses with 'literary aspirations', Selvon is able to orchestrate perhaps the first intentional and sustained parody of both traditional European, as well as contemporary West Indian, literatures in the history of West Indian scribal art. Literary allusion in *Moses Ascending* is therefore doubly organic, operating on verbal as well as thematic levels.

The literary echoes are overwhelmingly of vintage derivation. Moses and Bob are the late twentieth-century photo-negatives of Shakespeare's early seventeenth-century Prospero and Caliban. But this literary correspondence is not confined to Shakespeare; it extends to the work of George Lamming, who had consistently mined this classic culturo-political antithesis for the themes of his novels.[17] And just as Lamming has, in *Natives of My Person*, circumnavigated the themes of power and exploitation first launched in *The Castle of My Skin*, Selvon, by evoking the literary precedents of the master/servant motif,[18] obliquely recalls the historical origins of the 'black tragic' (105). And not satisfied with that framework, Selvon manipulates a mirror situation of human exploitation: West Indian 'Caliban', now turned guardian of the metropolitan language and trafficker in human cargo, finds himself 'in a quandary' over communicating with a Pakistani 'Caliban'!

> 'Speakee English!' I try.
> 'Fuck off,' he say, giving me a nasty look.
> It was not the most auspicious phrase in the Queen's language... (76)

explains the affronted Moses in pious outrage.

The Shakespearean motif is intensified by the sixteenth-century turns of phrase:

> I might of doffed my hat (105)
> let us away (105)
> If I had had time I would of said, 'Unhand me knave' (43)
> I could withstand the slings and arrows of misfortune (50)

Perhaps because of the novel's satiric content, and as a means of exploiting to the full the direct address of the first-person narrative technique, Selvon's literary 'word-hoard' tends appreciably to be eighteenth-century. The 'dear', 'gentle', and 'perspicacious' reader is ever so often formally invited to pass judgement or sympathise:

> Another point I would like to make in passing is the lack of social graces in Galahad. Note the invasion of my castle, note the intrusive, aggressive entrance ... note, I say, the stab at my Achilles heel! (47)

When Selvon relinquishes this period narrative style and its Classical reference, he may have recourse to Cromwellian expletive:

> I was thunderstruck. 'God's blood,' I cried...
> 'Hold your water,' Bob say. 'Cool it.'
> 'Cool it?' I mock him. 'Egad, man, they have really irked my ire now.' (105)

When one adds to this eighteenth-century linguistic flavour the resonances of Dick Whittington and his cat, and those of Robinson Crusoe's and Prospero's relationship with the 'natives' of the Caribbean, the dramatic and verbal ironies of the Moses/Bob association are evocative and complex indeed.

But Selvon, for all his banter of situation and discourse, can modulate his humour by cross-fertilising it with a mocking but serious tone, reminiscent of the 'picong' mode. One of his techniques in this regard is to replace the behavioural content of picong's oral address with allusion to literary precedents bearing sombre/pathetic overtones.

TEXT	ASSOCIATIONS
there was a tear in my eye (97)	Dickensian sentimentality
A man must go where the winds of fortune blow him, willy-nilly, for his Destiny is writ in the stars, nor all thy tears wash out a word of it. (74)	Omar Khayyam, *Rubaiyat*

Similarly, the meditative passages on the fate of impoverished black workers in England:

Where have they gone? What are they doing? Somewhere out there somewhere among the millions of whites; in the bustling traffics and the towering buildings and the confusion and pandemonium of the city, they are scattered and lost. I only hear stories of their plights and sorrows, tales of tragedy whispered on the wind… If you do not keep in touch with your friends and acquaintances you will think they are *dead* in this country. They vanish from your life; they go down in the underground and they never emerge; they are blurred into a crowd and become part of the density of humanity, individualistic only in a kind of limbo memory. (16)	*ubi sunt?* motif Medieval/Renaissance rhetorical 'figures' *Bible* the Gothic novel Eliot, *Wasteland* *Wasteland* *Psalms* Ellison, *Invisible Man* *Wasteland*

And so, by allusions both erudite, recondite, and sober in tone as well as by the rumbustious coinages, malapropisms and clichés of the self-educated, Moses emerges as a complex figure – of a type with the ironic portraits of Chaucer's *Canterbury Tales*, like the Nun and the Pardoner. As with them, the ironic content of Moses's tale operates not only within the text itself, but even more fully in relation to the personality and aspirations of the teller of the tale. In the end, it is as if the straining of the will to escape social determinism catapults him down, not unlike Milton's Satan, from his heavenly attic and ivory tower to the hellish basement, that twentieth-century equivalent of the 'hold of a slave ship' (43).

What this essay has tried to show is that the socio-historical tensions[19] underlying Moses's aspirations are reflected in the incongruity of his language codes,[20] in the concomitant severity and suddenness of his register shifts, in inconsistent grammatical forms, and in extravagant metaphoric comparisons. So that while Moses sometimes consciously creates humour for his readers by these means, his stylistic variations are not always controlled and he himself eventually falls victim to his own eclecticism, flamboyance, and striving for effect. So while language in *Moses Ascending* accounts for a large part of the humour in the novel, it is itself a metaphor of Moses's ambivalent, ambiguous and ironic situation. Yet despite his reverses of fortune, Moses can count it a success to have penned and published these inimitable Memoirs through the mediation of Selvon, his creator. In fact, both Selvon and his creature Moses (Prospero and Caliban) can justifiably boast: 'All have come, and see, and I conquered' (32).

1 See Errol Hill, *Trinidad Carnival: Mandate for a National Theatre* (Austin: University of Texas Press, 1972).
2 See Sandra Pouchet Paquet, 'Introduction', in *Turn Again Tiger*, by Sam Selvon (London: Heinemann, 1979); Michel Fabre, 'Samuel Selvon', in *West Indian Literature*, ed. by Bruce King (London: Macmillan, 1979) and 'Moses and the Queen's English', *Trinidad and Tobago Review*, 4:4 (Christmas 1980), pp.12-15, for thematic and structural affinities between Selvon's *oeuvre* and the calypso.
3 Trinidad terms: 'old talk' – gossip, trivial chat; 'mamaguy' – jovial flattering remark meant to provoke embarrassment and diffidence in its recipient; 'picong' – bantering, superficially approving remark masking

a negative comment, but expected by its sender to be received with jovial agreement and *bonhomie* or, at the minimum, with tolerance.

4 See Edward Brathwaite, 'Houses in the West Indian Novels', *Literary Half Yearly*, 17:1 (1976), pp.111-121; also *Tapia*, 3 July 1977, pp.5-6.

5 This motif seems to parody the confessional exercise of Kripalsingh in V. S. Naipaul's *The Mimic Men*.

6 A language style appropriate to a particular social, cultural, psychological, or professional context.

7 Samuel Selvon, *Moses Ascending* (London: Davis-Poynter, 1975), p.10. All subsequent references cite this edition.

8 Basilect, mesolect, and acrolect demarcate progressively the furthest removed through to the most approximate manifestations of dialect performance relative to its 'standard' or 'model' language, here Standard English.

9 See Donald Winford, 'The Creole Situation in the Context of Sociolinguistic Studies', in *Issues in English Creole: Proceedings of the 1975 Hawaii Conference*, ed. by R. Day (Heidelberg: J. Cross-Verlag, 1980).

10 See Donald Winford, 'Grammatical Hypercorrection and the Notion of "System" in Creole Language Studies', *Carib*, 1 (1979), pp.67-83.

11 Bearing in mind Naipaul's observation of offensive refuse at the most frequented bathing sites along the sacred Ganges in *An Area of Darkness*, 'the bonny banks of the Ganges' rings a farcical bell.

12 An echo of Biswas's nickname in Naipaul's *A House for Mr Biswas*. The Tulsi family satirised Biswas's independence by calling him 'the paddler' since he insisted on 'paddling his own canoe'.

13 The most socially acceptable dialect of British English.

14 There tends to be little or no dialect differentiation in Selvon's *oeuvre*. Apart from the Trinidad dialect-based discourse of the narrative voice, Selvon makes no attempt to realistically match character to dialect, whether in regard to lexical, syntactic, or likely register choices. In *The Lonely Londoners*, for instance, a Jamaican character – called by the non-Jamaican term 'Tanty' – speaks in Trinidad Creole. Selvon defends this strategy in Fabre, 'Moses and the Queen's English'. Similar inconsistencies occur in *Moses Ascending*. Faizull, a Muslim, requires to be cleansed by a 'pundit' – a Hindu term for a Hindu priest (76). And Bob, the Englishman, associates 'Bangladash' with 'one of them new African states' (39), using a Trinidad Creole noun-plural form.

15 Perhaps one of the first articulations of the perverse satisfaction de-
rived by West Indians from British discomfiture at the size of the non-
White immigrant influx since the 1950s is Louise Bennett's 'Coloni-
sation in Reverse'. See her *Jamaica Labrish* (Kingston: Sangsters, 1966),
p.179.

16 Fabre, 'Sam Selvon', pp.123-124. He sees this aspect of Selvon's work
as being in line with 'post-modern fiction… [uniting] the iconoclastic techniques of the West and the iconoclastic techniques of the calypso in order to liberate Trinidadian fiction by negating the monopoly
of the "great tradition".'

17 As Fabre states on p.124, *Moses Ascending* is 'a novelist's novel'. Through
Moses, Selvon makes several direct allusions to West Indian writers.
While covertly alluding to differences in tenor between their work and
his, Selvon approvingly recognises the work of two professional col-
leagues: Galahad disparagingly challenges Moses – 'You think writing book is like kissing hand. You should leave that to people like Lamming and Salkey' (46). On p.52 he signals his awareness – doubted
by some of his earliest critics – of 'plot, dialogues, continuity and other
technical points'. See also footnotes 5, 11, 12, 15, 18.

18 Other master/servant pairs paralleled by Moses and Bob are Cervantes's Don Quixote/Sancho Panza; P. G. Wodehouse's Billy Wooster/
Jeeves. The Robinson Crusoe/Man Friday motif has inspired the pivotal image in Derek Walcott's *Castaway*, and finds an oblique reso-
nance in the reiterated image of shipwreck in Naipaul's *The Mimic
Men*.

19 As well as his moral vacillation.

20 Although in some contexts 'code' and 'register' are synonymous, I re-
fer here specifically to Basil Bernstein's formulation and definition in
Explorations in Sociolinguistics, ed. by S. Lieberson (Bloomington: In-
diana University Press, 1966) of 'elaborated' code as a structurally complex and socially formal style of discourse in contradistinction to a 'restricted' code, which utilises a limited vocabulary, slang and other in-
formal expressions, in addition to simple or even incomplete syntactic structures, with meaning being communicated extensively through
extra-linguistic factors such as body language and understood context.

THE PHILOSOPHY OF NEUTRALITY: THE TREATMENT OF POLITICAL MILITANCY IN SAMUEL SELVON'S *MOSES ASCENDING* AND *MOSES MIGRATING*

VICTOR J. RAMRAJ

In his latest novels, *Moses Ascending* (1975) and *Moses Migrating* (1983), Samuel Selvon portrays a facet of the protagonist Moses that he omits altogether in *The Lonely Londoners* (1956), the initial volume of the Moses trilogy[1]: for the first time since migrating to London, Moses is confronted with political activists, full of passionate intensity, who are persuading him to take a stand politically and are making his life miserable by ridiculing his apolitical stance. In depicting Moses's experience with these activists, Selvon pokes fun in both novels at the politically zealous and militant, but his treatment of this theme varies considerably between the two novels. In *Moses Ascending*, he shows Moses besieged by Black and Asian militants who make him feel guilty because he steers clear of their radical actions, desiring to be left alone to 'live in peace' (3), practising a 'philosophy of neutrality' (97). Caught between commitment and passivity, he experiences excruciating ambivalence. When he briefly and naively experiments with political activism, Selvon employs him effectively as an ingénu to make fun of the militants. In the later novel, *Moses Migrating*, Selvon depicts Moses as now politically active himself – he is a self-appointed ambassador from Britain, committed to spreading British culture and proving British economic stability to his fellow Trinidadians. He is an eccentric, and his eccentricity becomes zanier and zanier as the novel develops. The author makes fun of his misconceived militancy, dissuading the reader from taking him seriously.

Selvon conveys his pejorative assessment of political zealots primarily through his skilful characterisation of the two Moseses, who, though they share the same name and several characteristics, are quite different individuals in their respective novels. They both have their origins in Moses of *The Lonely Londoners*. An important feature of Selvon's portrait of the early Moses is his relationship with Galahad, his close friend and fellow countryman, who appears as an important secondary character in the Moses trilogy. Reading the early novel in the light of the later novels points up Galahad's function as Moses's *alter ego*. Galahad, with whose arrival in London one dark winter night the novel begins, represents the antithetical aspects of Moses: he is positive while Moses is pessimistic, decisive while Moses is ambivalent, and active while Moses is contemplative and given to 'philosophising' and 'rhapsodising' (100). The two together suggest the classical dichotomy of the writer's psyche: the sedentary observer and the active participant. Galahad is not only a foil to Moses; he is a kindred spirit as well; and their oneness is recurrently underscored. On the first day of Galahad's arrival, Moses tells him in their shared Trinidadian English, 'I take a fancy for you, my blood take you' (21), and he subsequently admits to him, 'Ah, in you I see myself' (69) – a quotation that Selvon brought to my attention when I outlined my thesis to him.[2]

The three novels begin either with Moses's meeting with or parting from Galahad. *The Lonely Londoners* opens with their initial meeting, and *Moses Ascending* and *Moses Migrating* with their separation. Moses of *Moses Ascending*, who at the end of *The Lonely Londoners* is aspiring to be a philosopher-writer, tells the now militant, aggressive Galahad that this is 'the parting of the ways' (2). Moses has just bought a house and is leaving the basement he has shared with Galahad for many years for a penthouse where he intends to lock himself away and write his memoirs. He evidently wants to shed or suppress his Galahad traits. Galahad's response brings into prominence the oneness of the two and the futility of Moses's attempt to deny him: 'You can't erase me like that... I am part and parcel of your life' (3); and he warns Moses that to cope with the burgeoning militant political climate Moses will need him more than ever before: 'We shall see who needs who... I have noticed that you look as if you are ready to retire, but I am with it, man. You will need me to cope with current events and the new generation of black people…' (3). Moses spends the rest of the novel trying to avoid Galahad and to get his memoirs written; but Galahad is ever present, ever urging him to abandon the reclusive and contemplative life for the involved and militant. In one of Galahad's early attempts to coerce Moses into political involvement, he employs phrases indicative of his function as Moses's *alter ego*: 'I have to get through to you… It is my duty. If I got to spend the whole night here, I have to communicate. One of our troubles is that we don't talk enough, but I am going to convince you if it's the last thing I do' (12). Their oneness is further implied in Moses's allusion to *A Tale of Two Cities* when he is wrongly jailed – he was an innocent bystander at a Black Power confrontation with the police; he feels that Galahad should have offered to take his place, that is, Galahad should have played Sydney Carton to his Charles Darnay.

Galahad's and Moses's ongoing clashes externalise Moses's intensely ambivalent feelings. Ambivalence, as defined by Eugen Bleuler, the psychoanalyst who coined the term, is a human response in which the individual simultaneously or alternatingly experiences opposed attitudes and feelings toward particular people, places, or ideas.[3] Moses's behaviour in *Moses Ascending* perfectly illustrates this. His ambivalence is much more intense here than in *The Lonely Londoners*, where it is restricted to his love-hate relationship with London. Early in the later novel, his ambivalence becomes apparent in his passionate poetic outburst – which he describes as 'taking an objective view' (5) – on the pre-dawn labours that are exclusively the black man's in London.

> As he stands, mayhap, in some wall-to-wall carpeted mansion (resting, dreaming on his broom or hoover) and looks about him at mahogany furniture, at deeply-padded sofas and armchairs, at myriading chandeliers, at hi-fi set and colour television, as his eyes roam on leather-bound tomes and velvet curtains and cushions, at silver cutlery and crystal glass, at Renoirs and Van Goghs and them other fellars, what thoughts of humble gratitude should go through his mind! Here he is, monarch of all he surveys, passing the wine, toasting the Queen, carving the baron of beef, perambulating among distinguished guests, pausing, perhaps, for a word on the fluctuation of guilt-edge shares or the new play in the West End.
>
> And the black man is the chosen race to dream such dreams, and to enjoy the splendour and the power whilst the whole rest of the world is still in slumberland! Oh, the ingratitude, the unreasonableness of those who

only see one side of the coin, and complain that he is given only the menial tasks to perform! (As I became objective, I was mad to jump up and
put on my clothes and go straight to work!) (6-7)

The author clearly intends this passage ironically, but, as the last sen-
tence signals, Moses appears to be taking both literally and ironically what
he says here about the opportunities available to the blacks. Selvon pref-
aces the passage with this comment by Moses that sets in motion doubts
about the likelihood of unambiguous irony in the narrator-protagonist's
tone: 'One of the things that gave me great delight was to be able to stay
in bed and think of all them hustlers who had to get up and go to work'
(5).

   Moses has bought his house to achieve not just a form of independence – like V. S. Naipaul's Mr. Biswas – but social superiority as well. Cultivating snobbery and yearning to be the master, he believes that one of
the pleasures of becoming a landlord is being able to slam doors on pro-
spective tenants. Yet, there is much warmth to him. Though politically
uncommitted, he is humanly concerned with the lot of his fellow men.
One of the most moving passages in the book is his lament for his fellow
immigrants with whom he associated when he first moved to London –
as related in *The Lonely Londoners*:

> Where have they gone? What are they doing? Somewhere out there, some-
> where among the millions of whites; in the bustling traffics and the tower-
> ing buildings and the confusion and pandemonium of the city, they are
> scattered and lost. I only hear stories of their plights and sorrows, tales of
> tragedy whispered on the wind. I hear that Big City has gone mad, walks
> about the streets muttering to himself, ill-kempt and unshaven, and does
> not recognise anyone. It is as if the whole city of London collapse on him,
> as if the pressures build up until he could stand it no more and had to make
> a wild dash around the bend. (9-10)

What particularly endears this mildly eccentric narrator to the reader is
his constant self-examination – a quality which sets him apart from the
insensitive Moses of *Moses Migrating*. Moses of *Moses Ascending* is conscious of his eccentricities and apprehensive that he may be, as Galahad
harshly tells him, 'heading straight for the madhouse' (43). Angry with
Galahad on one occasion when Galahad dismisses his memoirs as the work
of a madman, he aimlessly walks the streets of London: 'And walking along

in a blind despair talking to myself, I suddenly realise I was doing the self-same thing that Galahad divine for me' (44).

Moses eventually accedes to Galahad's promptings that he put his memoirs aside and get in touch with reality by doing research on his black brothers and writing about the current sociopolitical scene. With this temporary surrender to Galahad, Moses's function in the novel undergoes a significant shift as he becomes the satirical ingénu. Armed with his notebook and clipboard, this novitiate activist gets himself into awkward racial and political situations in his effort to obtain material for his sociopolitical study. Selvon introduces the episodes relating these incidents less to define Moses's naiveté than to poke fun at the militants' narrowness, subterfuge, and biases. Moses is not really committed to his sociopolitical research, regretting that his work 'was suffering, and it didn't look as if I was writing my Memoirs so much as prognostications and a diary of current events. I longed to get back to my philosophising and my analysing and my rhapsodising' (100). In the end, he does write his memoir – which takes the form of the very novel *Moses Ascending*.

A Black Power leader's absconding with the Party's funds leads Moses to reassess his relationship with political activists. He undergoes an extended period of self-probing and makes a discovery that he describes in terms of an epiphany, though humorously: 'I suppose, really, this is what is meant when one sees the light, like how Saul become Paul. I try out Moses-Roses, and it come to me in a flash, like a revelation' (117). What Moses comes to realise is that he need not become a political militant to help his fellow men. Galahad is wrong: the solution is not in politics but in traditional values, in doing good to others, in being generous and philanthropic. Moses's philosophy is a romantic one, in keeping with his character that *The Lonely Londoners* defines as having 'the right feeling in his heart' (126).

The last two paragraphs of *Moses Ascending* address the politically militant, anticipating their misreading of Moses's memoir. Moses pointedly dismisses any political interpretation of his rise and fall as a landlord:

> One final word. It occurs to me that some black power militants might choose to misconstrue my Memoirs for their own purposes, and put the following moral to defame me, to wit: that after the ballad and the episode, it is the white man who ends up Upstairs and the black man who ends up Downstairs. (139-140)

And he concludes his memoir by announcing that he intends to regain his penthouse through the same means by which he lost it, that is, through sexual shenanigans rather than political militancy.

Moses's character undergoes a drastic change in *Moses Migrating*. He now has conceded to the Galahad part of himself – or, as he puts it, he has 'compromised' himself (2) – and is less contemplative, less bothered by inner conflicts, and less inclined to nurturing an inner life. The novel opens with him preparing to leave Britain – and Galahad – for Trinidad, and though initially he claims to be fleeing racial prejudice in Britain, as the novel proceeds, he perceives himself more and more as an ambassador of British culture and as an advocate of British economic and social stability. His plan to regain his penthouse from Bobbie and Jeannie, with which the earlier novel ends, is not followed up here. The novel is less a continuation of *Moses Ascending* than a separate work, even though there are brief initial references to some minor issues and situations in the earlier novel. Moses's political antics elicit farcical laughter. Selvon does not invite serious considerations of his views. Many of the characters, even some with walk-on roles, consider Moses to be mad or eccentric, and the reader tends to share their assessment. Here, for instance, is Moses's first meeting in their cabin with Dominica, one of his cabin mates, who, Moses assumes, is fleeing Britain:

> 'Aren't you ashamed of yourself?' I cried…
> 'What the arse you mean by if I ashame of myself?' he ask.
> 'You've made your packet, now you don't care about the hand that fed you,' I told him. He laugh. It was a kind of Caribbean laughter, derisive and mocking, what put you in your place. I was affronted. I stiffened.
> 'Man,' he say, 'you some sort of social worker or Welfare State or something?'
> 'I'm just a loyal Briton,' I say shortly.
> 'Oh,' he say, then 'Jesus!' and he laugh again. (25-26)

Dominica comes to the conclusion that 'Brit'n must of blow his brains' (31).

Galahad appears in the novel but only briefly at the beginning and towards the end. In the early pages, he functions briefly as a foil to Moses, but as the novel develops his function as Moses's *alter ego* diminishes since Moses in attitude and conduct is as much Galahad now as he is Moses. The polarised aspects of Moses's psyche have come together, as

Selvon shows in many of the incidents set in Trinidad where Moses is as cavalier and militant as Galahad. The Moses-Galahad integration is quaintly suggested by Selvon's equating Moses's prize, the Carnival Cup, with the Holy Grail; according to tradition, Sir Galahad was the only knight of the Round Table who succeeded in his quest for the Holy Grail.

The novel is as episodic as *Moses Ascending*, but, unlike that novel, most of the episodes are slapstick. Farce predominates. In describing Moses's trip to Trinidad, for instance, Selvon does not portray Moses pondering why he has decided to return to Trinidad or engaging in serious discussion with his cabin mates about what lies in store for them after so many years abroad – as would be expected of Moses of *Moses Ascending*. Instead, what the author emphasises about the journey home, in a long farcical episode, is Moses's and Jeannie's love-making in the same room where lies Jeannie's husband prostrate from seasickness. Similarly, the episodes set in Trinidad, such as the hilarious extended beach scene where Jeannie loses her bikini, are not intended seriously. In *Moses Ascending*, there are scenes of slapstick – the sheep-butchering scene comes to mind – but such scenes have thematic significance and are most important to the characterisation of Moses, who, armed with his pencil and clipboard, is making a conscious effort to become a student of the current sociopolitical scene. In *Moses Migrating*, Selvon has fun with his contrived plotting as well, particularly Moses's extremely fortuitous meeting with Tanty: he draws attention several times to it, chuckling each time he does so. The consequence of the contrived plotting, the numerous slapstick scenes, and the depiction of Moses as a zany eccentric is that Moses does not come alive and seldom engages the reader's sympathy, unlike his counterpart in the earlier novel. Samuel Selvon discourages taking Moses's frantic militancy seriously, playing it simply for laughter as an end in itself.

1 Sam Selvon, *The Lonely Londoners* (First published 1956; Harlow, Essex: Longman Caribbean, 1972); *Moses Ascending* (First published 1975; London: Heinemann, 1984); *Moses Migrating* (Harlow, Essex: Longman Caribbean, 1983). All further references are cited in the text.
2 Personal Interview, Calgary, Canada, 7 September 1985.
3 Eugen Bleuler, *Dementia Praecox, or the Group of Schizophrenics* (First published 1911; New York: International University Press, 1950), p.10.

COMEDY AS EVASION IN THE LATER NOVELS OF SAM SELVON

KENNETH RAMCHAND

———————————

The argument that in his later novels Selvon uses comedy to evade troubling issues depends upon a preliminary discussion of *The Lonely Londoners* (1956) where comedy is used for the opposite of evasion.[1] I am making the case in order to highlight a problem about Selvon's later work and if I tamper with my response and play down the 'entertainment' quality of *Moses Ascending* (1975) and *Moses Migrating* (1983) it is because the entertainment is the product of the evasion I want to explore.

*

In the closing pages (137-142) of Sam Selvon's *The Lonely Londoners* (1956), the central character thinks he sees 'some sort of profound realisation in his life, as if all that happen to him was experience that make him a better man'. It is one of the bases of the argument that Moses's process of growth runs through the novel and helps to make *The Lonely Londoners* come over to the reader as a book written out of belief in life's possibilities and belief in the thinking capacity which brings us into being: 'Still, it had a greatness and a vastness in the way he was feeling tonight, like it was something solid after feeling everything give way, and though he ain't getting no happiness out of the cogitations he still pondering, for is the first time he ever find himself thinking like that.' In this elated moment Moses's mind moves instinctively to the possibility of artistic expression.

He looks at a tugboat on the Thames 'wondering if he could ever write a book... what everybody would buy.'

This closing movement is convenient for the purposes of our discussion in another way: it embodies a positive view of the nature of comedy and the comic response; and it highlights crucial assumptions about the differences between comedy and tragedy as well as about the relationship between them. Here is Moses stumbling into truths as he reflects on the less happy-go-lucky side of the life of his fellow immigrants:

> Under the kiff-kiff laughter, behind the ballad and the episode, the what-happening, the summer-is-hearts, he could see a great aimlessness a great restless, swaying movement that leaving you standing in the same spot... As if, on the surface, things don't look so bad, but when you go down a little, you bounce up a kind of misery and pathos and a frightening – what?... As if the boys laughing because they fraid to cry, they only laughing because to think so much about everything would be a big calamity... (141-142)

Selvon's cast of vivid frustrated characters and his brilliant use of both a narrating voice and the reported voice of the reflecting character Moses help to present throughout the book concrete forms of the things that inform the mood of the passage quoted above: the thin line between comedy and tragedy, the silence and stillness at the disconcerting heart of noise and movement, the jarring objects just under the topsoil.

If the comic response in *The Lonely Londoners* is profound, it is so because almost every episode contains an acknowledgement and defiance of tragic dimensions ('they only laughing because to think so much about everything would be a big calamity'), and every comment of the narrating voice is heard as the wisdom of one who has seen and suffered all.[2] In the closing movement that begins 'The changing of the seasons, the cold slicing winds'(137), Moses remembers the Sunday morning get-togethers in his room, the longings in his heart, and hauntingly, the role his friends' more immediate distresses impose upon him: 'Sometimes, listening to them, he look in each face, and he feel a great compassion for every one of them, as if he live each of their lives one by one, and all the strain and stress come to rest on his own shoulders' (139).

Of course some of the comedy in *The Lonely Londoners* fulfils conventional expectations such as that comedy bases itself upon and makes criticisms of certain kinds of inconsistencies and/or incongruities in the behaviour of human beings in society; and that its common targets are hypocrisy and pretension. An easy illustration from *The Lonely Londoners* is the would-be Englishman Harris spouting his version of impeccable English:

> And when he dress, you think is some Englishman going to work in the city, bowler and umbrella, and briefcase tuck under the arm, with *The Times* fold up in the pocket so the name would show and he walking upright as if is he alone who alive in the world. Only thing, Harris face black. (111)

But even when the comic incongruities in *The Lonely Londoners* relate to behaviours indicated by the conventional phrase 'manners and morals', they do so in their own way, colouring them with attitudes and values drawn from the cultural and political background. An even greater point of difference is that the cultural and political context is a source of comic incongruity in its own right. Tanty's unbending parochialism and her 'ignorant' demand that everything in England should conform to what she is accustomed to in Jamaica produce a number of comic scenes that make us think seriously about her as an instinctive practitioner of 'cultural resistance'.

It can be generalised that many of the comic incongruities in *The Lonely Londoners* are drawn out of the cultural situation of colonised persons out of sync with places and values, and that this continues as a shaping influence in the later works. In this light, *Moses Ascending* (1975) is the story of a Black man wanting to pen a memoir about his successful career as an immigrant; and *Moses Migrating* (1983) is a pilgrimage or mock pilgrimage from Great Britain by a nostalgic Black settler returning 'home' for Carnival. The conventions of writing a memoir and making a pilgrimage are mocked and turned upon themselves. In the more spectacular *Moses Ascending*, language itself is challenged: a hodgepodge of registers and styles and accents and an a-chronological assemblage of lexical items are orchestrated into an extravagant, entertaining and unrepeatable *tour de force*. All of this is deliberate, and it is so deliberately subversive of literary and linguistic canons and their social implications that it can be deemed anti-imperial.

The theme I want to explore, however, is that in the two later novels featuring the Moses character, the enabling conviction of a healthy balance between comedy and tragedy does not seem to be so consistently maintained: the comedy moves in a vein of farce and burlesque that suggests, in the midst of late twentieth-century social and cultural flux, either cynicism or an agnosticism that can mock all sides of every question. It is noticeable, too, that the comedy is now broader and more sexually explicit, and it depends increasingly upon a simple if resourceful revelation of incongruity after incongruity.

I would hazard the intuition that the increased reliance upon broad comedy in the two later Moses novels, and the uncertainty of purpose in Selvon's expression of the loss of belief and intensity in the Moses character are a function of the author's own problems of belief (to put it moderately), not unrelated to his departure from England for Canada in 1978.

*

We can begin with the safe observation that while Moses in *The Lonely Londoners* is a character involved in a quest that engages both reader and author, the Moses figure in subsequent books is less introspective and questioning, and less of a believer in the idea of fulfilment than some of his words might have led us to expect. The Moses we become familiar with in the book of 1956 is similar to Tiger (*A Brighter Sun*, 1952) and Foster (*An Island is a World*, 1955). These are introspective characters thinking about the wide world, the nature of human existence, their situation as individuals in their particular social environment, and their place in the larger world: Tiger with his notebook and dictionary; Foster trying to get behind the arbitrariness of words; and Moses part of the group and standing apart from the group, cogitating. It is worth emphasising that in his first three novels, Selvon encourages us to participate in the protagonists' search for answers, and to believe with the characters that there are answers to be found.

The time gaps between *The Lonely Londoners* (1956), *Moses Ascending* (1975) and *Moses Migrating* (1983) would partly account for the fact that they do not exhibit the continuity of attitude that we see in Selvon's first three novels. If the Moses novels constitute a trilogy it is a trilogy that only serves to record, without accounting for, the progressive deterioration of the character called Moses over twenty-seven years.

The Moses who appears in *Moses Ascending* nineteen years after *The Lonely Londoners* claims to be the same person, only older, professing himself now to be above the lower orders and unwilling to get involved in other people's cases or causes. He has accumulated the money to buy a house and rent out rooms to others in the very city where he used to be at the mercy of landlords: 'I insert my key in the front door lock, I enter, I ascend the stairs, and when the tenants hear my heavy tread they cower and shrink in their rooms, in case I snap my fingers and say OUT to any of them.'[3] Ensconced in the best apartment that he grandly calls 'the penthouse' (we know that this near-derelict building is scheduled for demolition), he can play at being a dreaded English landlord, or act the Black Robinson Crusoe to his White manservant Bob ('a willing worker eager to learn the ways of the Black man').

Above all, however, Moses sees himself as a writer, and he is about to set to work on his Memoirs. He has already published a book about those colourful days in the 1950s (he is claiming to be the author of *The Lonely Londoners*) when he was 'mentor and mediator, antagonist and protagonist, father and mother too' to so many West Indians in the city, but all of that is 'done and finish with' (44). He wonders about 'the boys' from his hustling days. ('They vanish from your life; they go down in the underground and they never emerge.') But as he intends to enjoy his hard-won prosperity, he is not going to try and trace their whereabouts; he is sure that 'wherever they are, there would be a lurch, and they would want me to pull them out of it' (10).

When Galahad tries to interest Moses in joining the Black Power movement and being one of its financial backers, Moses resists: 'The thoughts that fill me was thoughts about how a man could wish he is just living his life, and how people want you to become involve, whether you want to or not' (14). As Moses continues to develop his point, he sounds for a tantalising moment like Tiger, Foster, or the Moses of *The Lonely Londoners* and not as someone who regards himself as having succeeded in the White man's world and who is anxious to distance himself from the ranks out of which he has risen: 'Why is it that a man can't make his own decisions, and live in peace without interference? It is enough trouble for me to cogitate on the very fact of being alive in this world, wondering what going to happen to me, if when I dead I going to come back alive again...' (14).

This is promising but as the novel develops, the 'cogitations' do not continue. This Moses seems to be incapable of any introspection at all, and cannot take himself seriously for long enough to produce sustained writing or thinking. When Bob, the White manservant, and his wife,

Jeannie, become the occupants of the penthouse, and Moses has been de-
moted to the basement, all that the shallow Moses can offer is: 'Thus are
the mighty fallen, empires totter, monarchs de-throne and the walls of
Pompeii bite the dust' (134).

If we think about him as a character in a novel we can say that Moses is
an older immigrant, settled but not secure, wary of revolutionary talk and
revolutionary posturings, and too threatened by the new ideologies and
prescriptions to be reliable in his judgements of them. He thinks he has
travelled further on the road to being British than his fellow West Indians,
and although he seems to have no choice but to associate with them, he
verbally sets distance between himself and them.

His conservatism is founded on insecurity. Early in the novel, when
Moses imagines that the police might have a case against him for provid-
ing a base for the Black Power organisation and for allowing his place to
be used as a transit house for illegal Asian immigrants, his fears of a return to horrors he thinks he has come through are absorbed in an evoca-
tion of the Black man's nightmare of police injustice and Sisyphean struggle in an everlastingly hostile environment:

> Ensconced in my penthouse and enjoying my hard-earned retirement, I
> had allowed my affairs to get out of hand. If things continued at this rate,
> I would soon be on the downward path, fetching and carrying, back to
> the old basement room in Bayswater and pigfoot and neck-of-lamb, and
> what-happening Moses…
>   …The experience of that policeman coming and knocking at my door
> and asking all them rarse questions had me depress. I don't know if I can
> describe it properly, not being a man of words, but I had a kind of sad feel-
> ing that all black people was doomed to suffer, that we would never make
> any headway in Brit'n. As if it always have a snag, no matter how hard we
> struggle or try to keep out of trouble. (34-35)

But when he has to surrender the penthouse to his White servant Bob, his
comments point in another direction. Moses is quick to warn the reader
not to identify him with Black militants who see the world as a place where
Blacks always end up as losers.

> It occurs to me that some Black power militants might choose to miscon-
> strue my Memoirs for their own purposes, and put the following moral to
> defame me, to wit: that after the ballad and the episode, it is the white man

who ends up Upstairs and the black man who ends up Downstairs. But I
have an epilogue up my sleeve. (139-140)

He is just biding his time, planning to get his own back by arranging for
Jeannie to catch Bob in one of his encounters with Brenda.

The Moses character in *Moses Ascending* is more inconsistent and more
situational than characters in life or fiction usually are, and the reader discovers the appropriate accommodation on recognising that Moses is more
an authorial device than a character being developed and explored. With
Moses as medium Selvon registers the following without necessarily sub-
scribing to Moses's opinions about them: the new generation called Black
British so different from their immigrant parents and grandparents; the
Asian incursions that are to have such an impact on British economy and
society; the meeting of cultures in a context where the native culture still
finds it hard to give up its sense of superiority; and race relations, including the growth of Black Power feelings and Black Power movements linked
to developments in the United States.

To this list we must add Moses's project to write a book. This allows
Selvon to insert in *Moses Ascending* a number of general notes from a writer's journal: how a writer writes or is distracted from writing; the relationship between writer and audience; and what the act of writing does
for the writer himself. More specifically, the book makes a number of references to works and writers dealing with the condition of Blacks in Britain in the 1960s and 1970s. Moses's discourses about writing touch upon
the difficulties of being a writer in an uncongenial environment, in this
case a West Indian writer of the first wave trying to practise his craft in a
rapidly changing London. The book might even be deconstructed to yield
up information about Selvon's personal struggles as a writer. But the medium through whom the discourse about writing comes is a literary fraud.
The commentator on social, cultural and political matters is a supporter
of the status quo.

To show up Moses as a literary fraud and an irrelevant writer, Selvon
allows other characters to comment unfavourably on his writing. We are
made to realise that Moses hasn't heard the names of Lamming and Salkey
(43), and in one scene, Selvon has Moses contemptuously kicking aside a
batch of *Water for Berries* (he gets the title wrong) to look out of the window.

The one extract from the Memoirs that we get to see is the previously published set-piece on Blacks working the London night-shift, cleaning offices and streets, and removing garbage (5-9). It is an accomplished piece of satirical writing about the continuing exploitation of the Black working person in London. But having infiltrated this, Selvon uses Brenda to criticise Moses's literary ambitions. The young Black British activist who runs a Black Power newspaper out of Moses's basement tells Moses to his face that he is a pretentious and bumbling word-paster, and she tears into the Memoirs for its hodgepodge of styles, its grammatical and syntactic traffic jams, and its utter incompetence as writing:

> 'The only sentence you know, Moses,' Brenda went on, delighting in my discomfiture and misery, 'is what criminals get. Your conjunctions and your hyperboles are all mixed up with your syntax, and your figures of speech only fall between 10 and 20. Where you have punctuation you should have allegory and predicates, so that the pronouns appear in the correct context. In other words, you should stick to oral communication and leave the written word to them what knows their business.' (104-105)

When Galahad sees the self-declared author of *The Lonely Londoners* at work on the Memoirs, he accuses him of being out of touch and of living in the Dark Ages, of not knowing that 'we have created a Black Literature'. According to Galahad, Moses should be writing about 'the scene today, and the struggle' (43), but he is too cut off from life and current activity to be able to do so.

The exchange between Moses and Galahad allows Selvon to set out two approaches to writing that bear upon the question of the artist's commitment. Galahad's question is a modern question: 'How you expect to stay lock up in your room, and don't go and investigate and do research and take part in what is happening, and write book?' Against this the aspiring Moses sketches a traditional approach as he delivers what he considers to be a crushing reply: 'Let me remind you that literary masterpieces have been written in garrets by candlelight, by men who shut themselves away from the distractions of the world' (43).

The second attitude seems to be more congenial to Moses. After being seduced into standing bail for some members of the Black Power movement, Moses complains that being drawn back into the world is frustrating his writing mission:

> What touch my soft spot most of all, of course, is that my work was suffer-
> ing, and it didn't look as if I was writing my Memoirs so much as prognos-
> tications and a diary of current events. I longed to get back to my philoso-
> phising and my analysing and my rhapsodising, decorating my thoughts
> with little grace-notes and showing the white people that we too could write
> book. But all that come like a dream the way how circumstances continue
> to pester me and keep me away from my ambition. (100-101)

On the other hand, when Galahad accuses Moses of irrelevance as a
writer, Moses's language is his own but there is a poignancy in the reflections as Moses ostensibly wonders whether the call for topicality can be
ignored:

> I try to put down a few words, but I couldn't write anything. I just sit
> down there, morose and dejected. Bob must of thought that I was going
> through one of those periods when the inspiration wouldn't come, that we
> scribes know so well, for he was very discreet and did not make a nuisance
> of himself. But in truth I was brooding. Suppose, just suppose, that there
> was an element of truth in what Galahad say? Suppose when I finish,
> and ready to present my Memoirs, nobody want to read them? Suppose he
> was right, and I should start to write about Black Power, and ESN schools,
> and the new breed of English what are taking over the country? And what
> about all them Pakis and Indians who swim across the Channel and sneak
> ashore, or hide in them big trucks what come from the Continent? (45)

Selvon's peculiar use of Moses to raise basic questions about the fate of
writing and about the peculiar situation of an older writer like Selvon in
the Britain of the late 1960s points perhaps to the author's own self-ques-
tioning.

I do not think Selvon quite treats Moses as a satiric butt and if we read
him as a satiric device we find that it is satire without even an implied
positive, satire that does not believe in norms. I prefer to point to the de-
generation and cheapening of comedy and argue that at its best *Moses Ascending* is the kind of novel in which such significance as there is comes
less from the implications of the comedy as in *The Lonely Londoners* than
from a teasing out of the topics Selvon wants to comment on, the things
that are said through him. The emphasis in other words is on the function of the character.

Although this is not a book about the character of the character, we are
given the necessary working sense of the character: an essentially confused

being, highly situational, self-deceiving and pretentious, whose actions are seldom consistent with what he wants or says he wants. These impressions are not inappropriate. For it is clear enough that *Moses Ascending* is a comic rendering of a frightening new topsy-turvy world (literally, a society straining to accommodate all the legacies of its imperial encampments now coming home to roost), a novel about a spreading disorder reflected in the state of Moses's language and in the flotsam and jetsam of his confused mind. The Moses of *The Lonely Londoners* disappears (we have seen that it is impossible to disappear without a trace), and doubt is sown as to whether the optimism of quests like his can be maintained in face of the busyness of the post-colonial and post-modern world.

The moment of illumination Moses experiences at the end of *The Lonely Londoners* belongs to a different order from the world in which the character has his 'moment of truth' in *Moses Ascending*, and the earlier work has no trace of the self-deflation and cynicism that run through the later one:

> What pleasure was I getting out of my landlordship or out of the blood money earned from the traffic of illegal immigrants? Where was the high life and the champagne and the invitation to the garden party in Buckingham Palace, driving up in my Rolls with the number plate BLACK 1, and the batman Bob chauffering? And even if all these things were added onto me, what were they but evanescent, hollow delights that could never still the poignant pangs of conscience? I flagellated myself... I suppose, really, this is what is meant when one sees the light, like how Saul become Paul. I try out Moses-Roses, and it come to me in a flash, like a revelation. Without further ado, dear R, let me say that after these sober reflections, I resolve to turn over a new leaf. (117)

The epiphany in the later novel is a mock epiphany, and Moses's tone and language betray his contempt for old-fashioned things like belief or value. For two or three days, Moses takes every opportunity to remind people that he is a reformed man. But the reader sees him working his way into a position to seduce Bob's new bride Jeannie. When Bob comes home unexpectedly and catches him in a compromising situation all he can do is offer to turn over the penthouse to the servant. Bob takes the penthouse in compensation and now plays the part of master. To the sexist Moses, this is the way the world goes, no issue of morality or betrayal of friendship arises. Bob too may talk about betrayal and infidelity but Moses knows it won't be long before Bob himself will do something that will allow Moses to catch him out and reclaim the penthouse. Selvon's ribald comedy in this novel has no system of belief or value to which it might attach itself and it looks as if, philosophically, the author too is close to the position that there are no norms.

*

Moses Migrating picks up where the previous novel left off. Moses has not been able to regain the penthouse, and he is afraid that the police might crack down on the basement out of which Brenda and Galahad are still conducting Black Power business. In this novel, the retreat from what the old Moses stood for goes further; the sexist attitude of Moses and the other males is rampant, and there is more sexual spice; and the houseboy attitude to British culture is in full bloom in the mimic-man form of a militant anglophilia. The pattern of growth and hope that ran subtly through *The Lonely Londoners* re-appears but only to be denied and devalued. Moses says that he wants to re-make his life but his soul-searching is superficial and in any case he is afraid of change; he has a 'mighty dread to disturb the pattern I had lived abroad: I was scared stiff to refamiliarise myself with anything'.[4]

This Moses has a philosophical position not unrelated to the sense many people have that there are no absolutes holding the world together, and no inevitable logic in human affairs. In the apparently relentless march of the world, people move from climax to climax and they have to make what they can of discontinuity and the lack of closure. This is how Moses puts it:

> ...[I]n real life one goes from climax to climax – one thing leads to another, as it were, and you have to apply yourself to the continuation of your existence. The onlyest thing I know that have one definite climax is fairy tales, because all of them finish by saying that they live happily ever after. (167)

For Moses, life is made up of a series of separate chains of circumstances each of which has a climax. Each climax is a possible moment of death but these moments do not build into any fiction of order or progression: 'When I look back on my life, I see many times when there was a climax to a certain chain of circumstances and events, when one would have gladly given up life. If one had the choice, would one opt for a demise in the past, or take pot-luck in the future?' (166).

The world has changed and Selvon's knowledge of what Moses is now talking about makes it hard to practise the comedy of *The Lonely Londoners*. It is evident that in *Moses Migrating* the philosophical Selvon of the early novels and of the early writings gathered in *Foreday Morning* (1989) wants to return. There are moments and movements, too, when we catch distant glimpses of the romantic Selvon, dreamer of possibilities, writer of the poems and of the lyrical short stories of the late 1940s and early 1950s. But the world has turned too much and Selvon can neither recover and hold for long the mood and passion of 'My Girl and the City', nor sympathise with the obsession of a Bart seeking his Beatrice, nor bring himself to return wholeheartedly to the sensibility of a Tiger, a Foster or the old Moses who saw 'some sort of profound realisation in his life'.

In his imaginary conversation with St Peter, Moses refers to one moment that he cherishes:

> Imagine being asked by St Peter at the pearly gates, after he show you a flashback, 'That was your life, my son. When would you have preferred to die?' I would say, 'You remember that Jouvert morning when I was with Doris in the hotel, St Peter?'
>
> 'Yes, my boy,' he might well reply. 'You have chosen well, for your life before that, and after that, was full of sin and transgression. It was your finest hour.' (166-167)

The Doris referred to by Moses is a young woman in Trinidad and the hotel is 'de-Hilton' where he deflowered her on Jouvert morning just a few days before his flight back to Great Britain. We note that if Moses cherishes this moment, it has not had any discernible outward effect on his life. The evasiveness this essay explores is to be seen at its height in Selvon's treatment of Moses's affair with Doris and of Moses's attitude to the land of his birth. The question is whether the distance between Moses and Selvon is sufficient. The supplementary query is whether in the presentation of Moses's attitudes Selvon is sometimes of Moses's party without knowing it.

It is not love of the island of his birth, nor disillusionment with the metropolis that brings a sadly departing Moses to Plymouth, the port from which he had caught his 'first glimpse of merry England' when he first arrived. What he feels now at the moment of departure is love for his adopted country. He is leaving with a heavy heart: 'I don't really want to go' he tells an immigration officer who cannot imagine that it is a loyal British citizen standing before him, 'I rather the bitter cold and the nasty smog' (24). But he owes love and duty to England. The British economy is sinking, and Moses, appalled that so many Blacks are abandoning his beloved country in its hour of need to return happily to the islands (25), takes it as his mission to show the outlanders in the Caribbean that 'the British bulldog still had teeth' that 'Britannia still ruled the waves' and that Britain was not only still on her feet, but was also 'the onlyest country in the world where good breeding and culture come before ill-gotten gains or calls of the flesh' (30). Moses means to visit Trinidad where he will be a missionary and a self-appointed ambassador of goodwill and good manners.

Working through the thoroughly colonised consciousness of this immigrant who has spent most of his adult years in England, Selvon's comedy makes play with all the emotions associated with the colonial's arrival in England (18) and with his departure therefrom (39). The scene of the native's return to his island is not so straightforward. The rhetorical questions Moses asks at the moment of arrival could only have been asked by someone with an insider's knowledge and feeling:

> When we sighted the tips of the Northern Range dappled in morning sunshine, did I stand at the rails with conflicting emotions to get my first glimpse of my native land after the years? When we pass through the Bocas into the Gulf of Paria, did I look up at the lighthouse on Chacachacare, and did I note the verdant little islands as we entered the harbour? Did I take a deep breath and sigh as the brilliant sun etched the houses and other buildings scattered about the hills around Port of Spain, and did I imagine myself falling on my knees and kissing the dear soil? (57-58)

The mock-lyrical is succeeded by the bathos of Moses's answer to his own question: 'None of that shit. I was sound asleep, having drunk myself into a stupor the night before' (58).

Is this a cynical attempt to suggest that all such emotions are spurious? Or is Selvon asking us to notice that Moses had got drunk the night before and that his perverse expression now is an indication of his fear of his own emotions and his reluctance to slip out of the groove of his London life? When the ship docks, Moses is reluctant to disembark: 'Sometimes you driving to some destination for some purpose, but you don't want to reach, you wish the drive could go on and on and don't finish' (58). When he checks in at the famous hotel he wonders 'what the arse I was doing here thousands of miles away from my tried and trusted surroundings, in a upside-down hotel' (60).

Aboard ship and in the early days in the hotel, Moses is a sexist lecher, a comic butt, and a self-deluding representative of the Queen. The comedy is coarse and broad, sexist and sexual. In the island Moses persists in the ridiculous pose of being defender of the faith, explaining to a Trinidadian reporter that Britain is still a great and powerful nation of whom the whole world is jealous (72); quixotically holding up to the staff of a café where a pay-first system is in operation, a model of trustworthiness and honesty in Britain where you are trusted to pay your money and take up a newspaper from an open news stand. In an inspired moment, he hits upon a project to enter and win the Carnival King competition parading a symbol of the Empire in the form of Britannia holding a trident on the face of a coin.

From about this point, the Moses character begins to take on another colouring. Bob's random suggestion that Moses needs time to himself to look up relatives and friends leads Moses to acknowledge to himself that he has no family in the island to come home to, and that he was in fact brought up as an only child. He becomes interesting in his own right as a character whose present attitudes and social formation an author might want to explore. But while Moses's situation has such possibilities, Moses's actual words about his childhood tend to suggest that the author wants to produce the easy predictable effects:

> Up to this moment, I have never told a soul the truth about my past, that I was born a norphan, and left to my own devices to face the wicked world, deposited on the doorsteps of a distant cousin in a old wicker basket, and nearly get tote away by the dustman and dump in the *labasse*. It was childless Tanty Flora, living alone, who took me under her wing and gave me the name Moses and brought me up, and told me the facts of life when I came of age... It does not shame me to confess my lowly origin: Christ himself was born in a stable. (61-62)

The reader may wonder whether Selvon's attempt at humour here is in complicity with Moses's refusal to look straight at his past and whether it is a tell-tale sign that Moses accounts for his loss of contact with Tanty by declaring in the next paragraph that up to the day he left London (as if he was counting) Tanty never wrote to him.

We can't help noting quickly that this cannot possibly have been the childhood of Moses in *The Lonely Londoners*. But this Moses attempts to re-establish links with Tanty, falls in love with the island girl, Doris, and becomes a character searching for roots and for a sustaining love in a desolate world. In the end, he flees from the island, Tanty, and Doris. The novel closes with him at the Immigration desk in a London airport holding proudly aloft the prize he had won for portraying Britannia in the Carnival Competition 'like Arthur Ashe hold up the Wimbledon Cup when he win the tennis, for all the peoples in the airport to see. Only to me it was like holding up the Holy Grail' (179).

From the moment of Moses's revelations about his past the reader is expected to enjoy the broad comedy and the bedroom farce while at the same time attending to the 'process' of the character. The two false analogies (Moses as King Arthur and Arthur Ashe) indicate the extent of Moses's cultivated blindness to the reality of himself, and would suggest that Moses is now the object of Selvon's irony and satire. But somehow this reader cannot feel that this is a conclusion towards which the novel has worked as to a climax. But let us look at how the process unfolds.

In his state of 'reminiscence and dim memories', Moses looks across the Savannah from the window of his hotel room. A motionless and lifeless mass on the pavement that he took to be 'a bundle of rubbish or something' discloses itself to be an old woman selling oranges. Moses and the reader accept Selvon's manipulation of chance and Moses rushes out to check on the miraculous apparition.

Moses's assiduously shored-up self-assurance is considerably shaken in the encounter with Tanty by the Savannah (62-68). They remember songs they used to sing when he was a boy, and Tanty (symbolically?) offers him a navel orange whose juice literally springs out as he begins to suck it. The reminder of the possibility of nurture and re-birth is followed, however, by a more recently built-up instinct:

> I began to rue my impulsive dash from the hotel. Not that I wasn't please to see Tanty, but it was as if out here by the Savannah I lose my identity and become prey to incidents and accidents: you remember that sanctuary thing I tell you about in London when I went for my passport, well, I feel the same way about de-Hilton. I wish Bob and Jeannie was with me, they would of sustain me with their presence, even make light of the encounter and push on to something else. (65)

The impulse to make light of the encounter is Moses's sin against his own possibilities. A little later, walking along Frederick Street (82-85) and feeling the sensation of being 'a bubble in a seething mass of humanity, where your life is not your own and you are powerless to direct your movements' Moses thinks of Tanty; then he begins to get 'my trio of adversities – restlessness, depression, and irritability'; then asks himself if it is really true that he is among his countrymen, knows no one, and has neither friend to look up, nor spot or place to remember: 'Alas, the answer was negative, and made more so by a mighty dread to disturb the pattern I had lived abroad; I was scared to refamiliarise myself with anything, I should have kept my arse quiet in de-Hilton, safe and secure among the foreigners and visitors' (84). Moses's fear eventually wins but in Selvon's account of how this happens the result seems quite arbitrary.

Moses's description of his first visit to Tanty's house in John-John (85-94) ends with Moses's declaration to himself and the reader that he is in love for the first time. As he makes his way up to the house through the section of the city in which he had grown up, Moses says that 'for the first time I begin to feel as if I come home in truth'. He is instantly attracted to Doris ('a strange bewitchment fall upon me from the moment I enter the door') and when she asks him if he has come back to stay he tells us that if she had indicated that it was her wish he would have been 'well and truly doomed', the reader at this point hardly noticing the words exactly. Later when Doris is sure that Moses would not give up his bed in the Hilton to spend the night on the floor in Tanty's house, Moses tells us that this is what he wanted to say 'I would sleep if you hang me up on a nail in the wall, just as long as Doris is near.' During the course of the evening, Moses learns that Doris's wish is 'to married a decent man and get out of Trinidad' but this does not frighten him off.

Walking back to his hotel after that first meeting, Moses is in love, by his reckoning:

> The sky was full-up of stars, and the air was fill with music of steel bands practising for the Carnival. I stump my foot on a junior boulder and didn't feel it. A anopheles mosquito sting me on my nose and I donated my blood without protest, so deep was I in thought, so deep the night. (94)

Although we chuckle at the 'junior boulder' and 'I donated my blood without protest', this is an effective intimation to the reader that Moses has fallen in love with Doris. In the next paragraph, however, Moses's language begins to move towards slackness, drawing a little more attention to itself, and playing to the reader much more than the preceding paragraph does:

> I used to hang out in Piccadilly Circus night after night, by the Eros statue, contemplating women from all over the world, and the little cherub Cupid never shoot me with his bow and arrow. The bastard wait until I come quite to Trinidad, up on John-John hill, to fire at me. (94)

The reference to England and Piccadilly Circus suggests the colonised Moses's preference, in theory, for beauties not from home, and his allegorical mode may be an indication that he is still unwilling to admit his condition to himself in plain terms. But a coarseness that is never absent from Moses's utterances and an impulse to amuse, impress, shock or bring the reader back to earth with expression itself turn up in the third paragraph: 'If I did know that arrow was coming, I would of duck instead of getting fuck, but it hit me square and fair in the middle of my heart' (94).

Of this passage and many others like it in the book, this question may be asked: are the trivialising effects in the language of the accounts a function of Moses's wish (conscious or unconscious) to deny or escape, or are they inserted to serve Selvon's determination to keep up the entertainment even if the entertainment serves to dissipate the seriousness of the issues? It is a difficult issue to decide, for two main reasons. Part of the evidence – the language Moses uses to describe his feelings – may be inadmissible: the language Moses uses is Moses's language, and cannot technically be deemed to be the author's voice. In the second place, an argument that an author evades the challenge and logic of the situation he has created runs the risk of turning out to be a declaration that he did not write the book one wanted him to write.

Perhaps the most convincing and satisfying of the passages in which Moses tells about his love for Doris is the one (103-108) that describes his second visit to the house and his first date with Doris ('a happy night, the happiest night in my whole life'). It begins with Moses bringing roses and a poem for Doris, a meal in Tanty's house, and the old lady's blessing of the liaison; continues with the visit of Doris and Moses to a calypso tent followed by a walk round the Savannah for coconut water and oysters; and ends with the walk back up John-John hill, after which Doris grants permission to Moses to kiss her hand:

> The steel bands in the neighbourhood was serenading we, and not with no rudeness calypso either, but something from the classics, a little light music, as it were. She said she got to get to know me better before I grant you any kisses, Moses, but you may kiss my hand if you wish. And that's how I know our love was the real thing, for in London, you only have to give them girls a bun and a cup of tea and they want to push their tongues down your mouth to tickle your tonsils. (108)

A little bit of bad taste comes in at the end of the paragraph, but this is Moses's most courageous and responsive moment. Moses's behaviour after his first meeting with Doris is the behaviour of a person in love, and he recognises that it is because he is in love that he can break an old habit and resist Jeannie's offers. He even takes the chance of confiding in his one-time crony the hard-bitten Galahad that 'I have fallen in love and I am actually contemplating marriage, which shows you it is no laughing matter' (156).

One of the sources of the comedy in the novel is Moses's obsession with the image of himself as a patriotic Briton with a duty to keep the flag flying. But being British is also Moses's prop or mask for survival. And it is the conflict between this prop and the risk of the new feeling that the novel seems set to explore. We have already noticed how from the first meeting with Tanty, Moses feels a threat to his adopted identity (65). When he falls in love with Doris, a theme of self-discovery begins to change both Moses and the tone of the book. The island woman is a challenge to him to find the real self beneath the role self. To accept Doris and the island is to end the pretence of being an Englishman, and to find a way to unite all the natives of his person.

Moses's extravagant dream of an estate in the countryside, a townhouse round the Savannah, two cars and a teetotal chauffeur might be a sign that he is not ready for the realities of living in the island. His elation when Doris agrees to assist him in preparing for the portrayal of Britannia on Carnival day suggests that he does not understand that he must choose between Doris and Britannia. 'I had a deep sense of joy and gladness as I realise I was fulfilling my two most important desires at one time, Britannia on one side, Doris on the other, and yours truly in the centre. We three were not a crowd' (115). Moses's failure to rise to the challenge of Doris and the island is a foregone conclusion given his interpretation that portraying Britannia at the height of the Trinidadian national festival is a way of proclaiming that Great Britain is still great. 'We three was not a crowd', but in due course Moses chooses Jeannie rather than the brown-skinned Doris to be the handmaiden to his Britannia on Carnival day.

But until the moment when Moses backs away from his intention to speak plainly to Doris the book encourages the reader to think that Moses will achieve clarity. Deciding that the time has come 'to tell Doris the story of my life' Moses invites her out to the gallery only to find himself hesitating. He makes excuses but eventually tells himself why he was unable to speak:

> I stood up there in the gallery in John-John, and for the first time – maybe second or third – I was at a loss for words, so delicate were my feelings. Also my ardour to open my heart was being cooled by the night breeze and the mosquitoes that was now ganging up and attacking in twos and threes; to boot, Doris make a joke and say they like my blood more than hers. But above all that to be quite honest, it was some primitive instinct, even stronger than my new-found emotions, that bade me be wary and don't rush in like a fool where angels fear to tread. (118)

The moment is lost and the disappointed Doris is not taken in by Moses's attempt to retrieve the situation ('What can I say to save the day?') by telling her that he has initiated plans to sell his property in England. Doris has been told by Tanty to measure Moses for his costume but she has begun in earnest to measure him as a man.

When Moses chooses Jeannie to be the handmaiden accompanying him in his portrayal of Britannia and wants it explained to Doris that he is doing so in the interest of authenticity; that he owes this to the country that took him in and nursed him all these years; that he is like knights of yore who must follow the path of honour and duty, and she must be like the wife of those times and submit to the inevitability of the situation, the reader is amused, but Doris does not see the joke. She begins to understand the chronic instability of the man who professes to love her. So, later, when he reproaches her for having an off-hand attitude towards him and serves notice of an intention to have a serious talk with her when the Carnival is over, Doris makes explicit what is now more than an intuition. Moses's life has been just a series of roles he finds it congenial to play: 'Your Carnival will never over, Moses. You are playing mas all the time' (151).

I am by-passing the comedy of situation, and the almost continuous incongruity between language and situation to focus on the emergence of a serious theme calling for a development of the character of the character. This alters *Moses Migrating* to the extent that while comedy and the other dimensions corresponding to tragedy exist in this book, they do so not as different faces of the same coin (as they are in *The Lonely Londoners*) but as two quite separate aspects of reality and as two intentions having nothing to do with each other.

The book is sceptical about the structure we attribute to reality and about the capacity of our fictions to create order and pattern. Its deflating of the emotions associated with so many sacred moments in a life (departure, arrival, falling in love, belief, etc), and its revelations of pretence and pretension give flesh to a cynical view of human affairs. But Selvon does not seem to know what to do with the reality seen in the beauty and dignity of Doris, the kindness and strictness of Tanty, and above all in the power of the love that overwhelms Moses even while he does his best to deny it. The presentation of the Jouvert morning episode when Moses makes love to Doris in the hotel helps us to complete the argument.

Doris has steeled herself to act on her understanding that Moses will never lay aside the mask and be his real self. Moses meanwhile has lost patience. He does not think it fitting that he should go to John-John hill and plead with Doris:

> Then I got to thinking why the arse I should have to plead, surely I deserved some sort of reciprocation for giving my heart away? I was using the wrong methods with her. I should be manly and forceful instead of hanging on her every whim and fancy. All I was doing was spinning top in mud, getting no place with all this romantic shit like a starry-eyed idiot, when I should give her the old one-two-three and use some Trinidad tactics. (161)

Moses proceeds to inveigle Doris to jump up with him on Jouvert morning. Under the influence of the ritual, both characters give way to what is their hearts:

> And in truth, I don't know what came over me that morning, if memories of bygone Jouvert return after all my years in stuffy old Brit'n, or if it was that I was in the midst of my countrymen now, the pulse and the sweat and the smell and the hysterical excitement, but my head was giddy with a kind of irresistible exultation like I just got emancipated from slavery. (164)

Moses proposes to Doris (165) and Doris proposes to Moses (166) but the author contrives that they cannot hear each other above the din.

The contrivance in this scene is not as acceptable as the contrivance by which Selvon allows Moses to find Tanty. If the purpose of the contrivance had been the comedic one of creating a misunderstanding to be resolved at the end when all's well that ends well, the contrivance would have been allowed to pass without comment. But the misunderstanding here does not get resolved. It is asking too much of the reader in these circumstances to accept that two adults who want to do something like proposing to each other can be so completely frustrated by a little carnival music.

An examination of the relationship between Moses and Doris establishes that what happens on the street is not carnival madness. The message of the novel so far is that if it is madness, it is madness that means to show them that it would be madness for them not to be together. In an earlier episode, Doris had told Moses that no man had touched her and no man ever would 'unless we join in holy matrimony!' Although she goes back to the hotel with Moses, she sleeps with him with misgivings ('I don't want to do it, Moses, I really don't') but this cuts no ice with Moses who reports, 'I deflowered Doris that Jouvert morning in my room at the hotel' (166). While Moses is sleeping it off, Doris slips wordlessly out of the hotel and Moses chooses to interpret her action as meaning that she subscribes to his philosophy that it is only fairy tales that have one definite climax 'because all of them finish by saying that they live happily ever after' (167).

I am arguing that what started off in *Moses Migrating* as a parodic treatment of the theme of return bears a striking resemblance to the real thing in the latter part of the novel until Selvon unaccountably cancels it.

Ash Wednesday evening finds Moses mounting up the hill to John-John, 'in a miserable pitiful state, my feet like lead, my heart heavy' (178). There is no music in the air, the sky is painted grey and deep purple. The scene is unsatisfactory in the sense that Doris and Tanty act as if Moses has done an irreparable wrong and Moses concurs in their judgement. But there is no verbal confirmation of this and obviously no discussion or explanation or attempt at apology:

> 'Tanty don't wish to say goodbye. That's why you come ain't it? She say she would pretend it was somebody who masquerade for the Carnival as you.'

'I better go inside.'

'No, Moses she don't want to see you, she say Carnival time everybody dress up as somebody else, that it's not real. I think so too.' (178)

Doris's earlier use of masking imagery in relation to Moses is now fully justified. To Tanty and Doris, he is an incorrigible role-player. As he moves slowly down the hill, he feels 'like Peter must of felt when he deny Christ' (179). The next scene discovers Moses at Heathrow Airport being checked by Immigration officers and holding aloft the prize he has won for his loyal interpretation of Britannia and deluding himself that this makes him a modern hero.

Selvon leaves us at the end with the Moses for whom playing carnival is never over. This man is always 'playing a mask'. But there are convincing traces in the novel of a Moses who could have stayed in the island with Doris. And there is also in the novel a Moses who feels like a man who has betrayed the Christ in himself. It is true that these latter possibilities have to be built up out of traces, and their credibility is limited at times, though not all the time, by the comic/cynical tone. But I think it is still safe to say that the challenge of the situation Selvon has created is not met by the ending that the author uses to close off the work. And I want to risk the suggestion that it is not only Moses who is being evasive. It seems to me that in *Moses Ascending*, and *Moses Migrating*, Selvon's comedy, delightful as it is, chooses an easy course that serves more to repress or deny the other face of the coin than to suggest the possibility of harmony and balance.

---

1 Sam Selvon, *The Lonely Londoners* (Harlow, Essex: Longman, 1985). All references are cited in the text.

2 For an extended discussion of the use of the narrating voice and the reported voice of Moses see my 'An Introduction to this Novel' in the Longman edition of 1985.

3 Sam Selvon, *Moses Ascending* (Oxford: Heinemann, 1984), p.4. Further references are cited in the text.

4 Sam Selvon, *Moses Migrating* (Harlow, Essex: Longman, 1983), p.84. Further references are cited in the text.

THE ODYSSEY OF SAM SELVON'S MOSES

JOHN STEPHEN MARTIN

In Sam Selvon's trilogy of *The Lonely Londoners* (1956), *Moses Ascending* (1975), and *Moses Migrating* (1983) the protagonist named Moses undertakes a journey that spans more than thirty years.[1] He travels from Trinidad to England, England to Trinidad, and thence back to England. Ostensibly, the novels deal with Moses's desire to enter the 'promised land', England. Like his biblical namesake, Selvon's Moses can never arrive, but spiritually neither can he go home.[2]

Moses is prevented from arriving at his new home by a systemic racism and caste structure that pits white against black, 'mother country' against 'colony', and 'have' against 'have-not'. The major studies of Selvon's fiction are so agreed on these themes that they focus on Selvon's use of dialect[3] and satire to depict their presence.[4] Such readings of an excluded minority, as noted by Edward Said, seemingly call for a nationalised 'oppositional criticism in its suspicion of totalising concepts' that might find a universal meaning to such specific confrontations.[5]

However, we have Selvon's word for it that such divisiveness and its resultant sorrows are not the goal of his fiction. Selvon advises us to look beyond the facile view that 'Third World writers can only produce novels and poetry of protest, or rattle the chains of slavery,'[6] and to consider instead that 'deep in their hearts all men think alike, it's only that some cannot express how they feel.'[7]

Because of this broader view, Ken Ramchand has called Selvon:

a philosophical novelist, not in the sense that he is using the novel form to
explore philosophical issues, but in the sense that he is creating characters
who, with varying degrees of articulateness, are trying to find out what their
own lives are about.[8]

It is this philosophical element that transforms Moses's life from a failed
journey to a 'promised land' into a parody of an odyssey. Moses hopes to
find a home in space, not realising that home is within himself, and is
different from what he initially envisioned. Thus, the immigrant journey
to a new land turns out to be an ironic odyssey about coming home to
what one's self is. To be sure, the odyssey is never-ending because one's
self is in constant reaction to what one finds at any moment.

The basis of this irony is in the narration of the three novels. In the
first novel, an unnamed narrator, a fellow Caribbean, tries to puzzle out
Moses's thinking after ten years of immigration; in the last two novels,
Moses himself narrates his own story , but he does not express all or get his
story straight. Moses, thus, is an unstable verbaliser of his own life. As a
result, faced with inconsistencies, the reader must constantly change his
interpretation of who Moses is. What the reader faces is a binary gamesman-
ship between two inconsistent points of view, the narrator's and his own.

At the opening of *The Lonely Londoners*, Moses is presented as having
waited to arrive in the 'promised land'. As he waits in Waterloo Station
for a boat train of newcomers, one of whom he is to shepherd into the
jungle of London, he shows that he is equally upset that Tolroy, a Jamaican who has come after him and whom he has helped, has sufficient money
to send for his mother. But when Tolroy discovers that not only his mother,
but his aunt, sister, brother-in-law and their children have also come, Moses
laughs as he thinks how Tolroy will have to face a financial burden as great
as the day he first arrived.[9] For the moment, Moses can rejoice that he is
not as vulnerable as Tolroy, having no family and thus no home.

Is Moses enjoying what Germans call *Schadenfreude* – a pleasure at the
dismay of others? It seems so. If so, the immigrant notion of arriving is
treated ironically. Laughing at Tolroy's burden of home, Moses can thereby
imply his own claim to having arrived in England.

No sooner than this binary play is over, another begins. Moses is upset
that the expected newcomer – the bizarre Henry Oliver who arrives in
the dead of winter sweating in his tropical clothes – does not accept his
condescending offers of help to get on in the white man's London in which

Moses believes that he is 'a veteran'.[10] Moses has a night job to get a few pounds more than someone at the bottom of the system might earn, but at the same time he denies that he has materially advanced himself. Faced with an outsider, however, Moses's need to maintain his self-image of arrival is so intense that he does not suspect any hypocrisy in asserting a 'blood' kinship for the new arrival even as he manoeuvres for superiority.[11] When Henry refuses Moses's offer of aid in order to show that he too is adept at arriving, his refusal challenges Moses's self-image as the 'veteran'.[12]

It is a complication that compels Moses to act perversely. After Henry sets out for the job centre, he soon panics on the street, almost fainting at one point after speaking to a constable. At this moment, Henry sees Moses approaching him, and he feels a spontaneous surge of friendship for Moses, different from what he felt earlier; impulsively, he opens up to Moses, using the Caribbean term 'boy' to signify their bonding.

As happy as the scene appears, it remains ironic. Although the newcomer Henry suddenly feels at home with Moses, Moses himself, it seems clear, has been following Henry, waiting for this very moment in which Henry must acknowledge his need for him and cease what Moses calls his 'big talk'.[13] For a brief moment, Moses has his sought-for companionship, but he surely has a tricky heart, deceiving himself and others because of his own loneliness.

In sum, then, life in London has transformed Moses. He does not see that his companionship comes ironically from raising himself above his fellows, the very persons who might make a home for him abroad. Moses experiences envy, the loss of dignity, and the existential mystery of life's vicissitudes without any hope of cessation. This ever-shifting situation is his spiritual home to which he must become accustomed, but whose existence he would constantly deny.

When Moses finally sees the fate of his fellows in London, he becomes indirectly aware of his own transformation. At the end of the novel, after ten additional years, Moses is walking in a park and sees Henry Oliver whom he has nicknamed Sir Galahad because of his apparent resistance to adapting to England's climate and racism. The irony of Galahad's transformation leads Moses to fancy that he might be a writer to tell Galahad's and the other boys' stories. However, to be sure, such stories would mirror his own, which he surmises has a 'greatness and vastness'.[14]

As a metafictional device, the narrator can say that Moses has stories to tell, which may be the events to which Moses reacted so impulsively throughout the novel. However, Moses cannot grasp that in telling them he would imply the telling of his own story of exclusion, and this telling would reveal his painful transformation and thus complete his spiritual odyssey home. Instead, here, the posture of writing may well be merely a necessary means of self-deception, of noting the transformation, but only in others.

This ironic pattern of complicated responses continues in the other novels. In *Moses Ascending*, Moses postures as a successful landlord of a desirable tenement in Shepherd's Bush, catering to illegal immigrants and Black Power activists.

Ironically, the tenement belongs to Tolroy who was set back financially ten years before when he brought in his family. Now Tolroy is emigrating back to Jamaica, and his decision is clearly ambiguous. Tolroy's return seems to be a synecdoche for the situation of the unique immigrant who has achieved a sense of home so that he no longer need seek a 'promised land' geographically. It is a synecdoche that tantalises Sam Selvon in all his novels.

Now, supposedly, Moses can assert his arrival because he evidently has made some money, despite all his complaining. Not only can he occupy the topmost flat – termed 'the penthouse' – but Moses, in parody of Defoe's novel *Robinson Crusoe*, can hire his own Man Friday, the white man from the Midlands, Bob, to be his menial. Moses relishes his position to give orders and teach the illiterate Bob to read. He also casts off his old hangers-on who would consider him a soft touch, particularly Galahad, who has become a streetwise Black Power activist.

However, despite his posturing, Moses cannot escape the binary play of impulse and subsequent verbalisations. He involves himself with the Black Power movement to ingratiate himself with a young ideologue, a writer of the group's newsletter, the beautiful and sexy Brenda. Even so, he is unexpectedly shocked by the unprovoked violence of the police and their dogs that break up a group meeting.

Moreover, although Moses reacts to this shock with some fervour, he grows disgusted with Bob and also the Black militants, Galahad and Brenda. He learns that Bob, his menial, also attended the meeting, and has been bitten by a dog; with such notice, Bob has become intent on having his picture in the movement's newsletter in order to cultivate Brenda's good feelings. What disgusts Moses with Bob, ironically, are the same urgings that have motivated himself.

Who is the real Moses? The reader cannot be sure. The reader only knows that Moses tells us things which he soon contradicts.

In the end, the reader must fill in the gaps of the story caused by Moses's contradictory assertions and responses. Thus, when Galahad says that Moses's much-touted Memoirs will serve him as a 'diversion', Galahad implies that Moses has lost his way and can only posture about his life. Evidently Galahad has hit the mark, for Moses takes offence at this, and the reader will recognise the familiar pattern of Moses's denying what is true and then setting about to contradict the recognition by action.

Thus the reader will see that Selvon's sharpest irony is reserved for Moses's treatment of Bob. Moses is intrigued by Bob's vanity, and although he admits briefly that he shares the same vice of womanising, he does not cease to plot. Indeed, Moses has become unhappy with Brenda because of her ideological verbalisations, but still he will not give up his interest in her because of his own sexual vanity, and so he acts as if he had the right not to share her with Bob. As a result, he fakes a love letter from Bob to an old girlfriend from the Midlands, Jeannie, in order to get him out of the tenement. Moses's fine letter is a testimony of his ability to put on hypocritical attitudes at will and to write with sufficient skill to manipulate the less-educated. The reader, to be sure, must admire how the letter transforms a meaningless act of lust years earlier into a basis of marriage at the present time.

Bob, tricked as he is, touts his own 'ascension' by virtue of having a wife and a newly acquired literacy (thanks to Moses's condescending act of Crusoe-like nobility). However, when he catches Moses 'washing' Jeannie's back in her bath (as it is euphemistically termed), Bob reacts with the assumed morals of an offended English gentleman. So strong is this moral puffery that Bob can become the master of his landlord, Moses. As recompense for his injured honour, Bob stays on in the penthouse which Moses initially allowed him to use as a honeymoon suite, and insists that Moses henceforth call him 'Robert'.

Moses, in turn, must go to the basement where he shares quarters with the Black militants who would challenge his posture as a landlord allied to the white power structure. Knowing that he cannot find fellowship with the activists, Moses, in the last paragraph, plots his revenge on Bob, his slave-become-master, in the mode of a Jacobean drama:

> But I have an epilogue up my sleeve. For old time's sake Robert still knocks one with Brenda on and off. What I plot to do is to go up top, and not only inform Jeannie of his infidelity, but arrange for the both of we to catch Master Robert in *flagrento delicto*, when I will fling down the gauntlet. (140)

Almost as if lisping the name 'Robert' (instead of 'Bob') and using words of unctuous gentility, Moses shows himself to be as vain and morally blind as Bob. Instead of a journey to the 'promised land' of England, the journey has driven Moses back upon himself to face the chaos of his own spirit. Ironically, Moses shows by the passage that he has been anglicised sufficiently even if he cannot assert his arrival. This middle kingdom, then, is Moses's true home, if he only would recognise it.

In these two novels, Selvon has parodied the biblical Moses who cannot enter the 'promised land'. It is the final novel, *Moses Migrating*, that tells of Moses's Odysseus-like attempt to return to his Trinidad home after almost three decades of subtle anglicisation. Moses plans a visit as an opportunity to posture as an anglicised colonial who can show Trinidadians what it is to be British. He thus would enjoy the pretence that he has 'arrived' in the 'promised land', England, to those who remained at home. Travelling with Bob and Jeannie as tourists, Moses has a tourist's plan to drink rum punch and enjoy the Lenten Carnival as an outsider might, and thereby confirm his anglicisation.

Again, a reader finds instances of the binary game of impulsive self-pretensions and verbalised-or-not recognitions. Moses can play being British except to a fellow from Dominica, whom he calls Dominica. Dominica laughs at Moses's imposture and, indeed, all discrepancies and shams, even his own. Moses condescendingly would like to call Dominica typically Caribbean, but 'the Dominica laugh' is a signal for the reader to surmise the gap between Moses's words and his impulses, feelings, and beliefs. The laugh can mock others, as Dominica mocks Moses; or it can give one support even in a moment of recognition of one's deception.[15] For example, as Moses sees Tanty Flora, who took him in as an orphan and is the only family he has in Trinidad, his first words, in place of a greeting, accuse her of not writing to him for almost twenty years. She has continued to sell oranges on the street, and now she is old and does not respond easily; but when she does, she is sharp-witted, and at three points of the same conversation she lambastes Moses for not writing to her.[16]

There is no rebuttal by Moses, the sole narrator, and it becomes clear that he has been misleading the reader because he finds it more comfortable to mislead himself at times than reveal his problem of spiritual identity. In his effort to silence Tanty Flora and himself, Moses first attempts to do 'the right thing' as a British colonial, and so he talks condescendingly of her small, modest home. In response, she accuses him of talking like 'white people' (65). When Moses offers Tanty money for her oranges so that she can be free to go home, she is insulted because she does not consider selling to be work, and violently turns away the English pounds.[17]

With all these turns, a reader can imagine fully what Moses's long silence in not writing home implies. He has become sufficiently anglicised, just as he wished, but can only see this transformation, as ambiguous as it is, when faced with his roots. It is a troublesome situation, and to break off Moses promises to visit her in her old home, closing with the remark, 'and I make the Dominica laugh' (68).

The irony becomes more complicated when Moses does visit Tanty, and meets Doris, the only woman he ever loved and with whom he considers marriage. So intent is he on showing the best of being British to Tanty and Doris, that he designs a masquerade of himself as Britannia for a float in a contest in the Lenten Carnival. He must be bronzed as the figure on the old English coins; Jeannie becomes his white hand-maiden; and Bob, who pulls the float, is blackened. The local paper, the *Trinidad Guardian*, loves the float because it portrays Trinidadians after independence as masters and deniers of the hitherto 'promised land'. But Moses also loves the float because he believes that he can display the self-esteem which has for so long eluded him: he can see himself as a Brit with willing British subjects displaying the old pomp of imperialism which attracted him to England years before.[18] Ironically, Moses's self-image requires the enslavement of his former masters.

Britannia is an illusion, an ambiguous one. It signifies why he cannot stay in Trinidad and marry Doris. Doris tells him on his goodbye visit, Tanty 'don't want to see you, she say Carnival time everybody dress up as somebody else, that it's not real. I think so too' (178).

As Moses himself says, life is a movement of 'climax to climax' (167) which reflects a web of illusions, arising from the heart's impulses. This is how he has lived in London, and this is what his pretence of Britannia confirms: he cannot change, even when faced with his roots, simple and direct as they are when represented by the two women.

As a consequence, Moses has nowhere to go but back to England, the home of the transformed immigrant he is. However, his return – as a final irony – is virtually as a newcomer, undermining his pretences of thirty years. At the close of the novel, Moses comes to Heathrow, waving about the Cup received for winning the masquerade as Britannia. Moses assumes that he is behaving as a British sports fan, but the immigration officer who takes Moses's passport to the back for a closer check evidently sees Moses misbehaving as a stereotypical black. The situation is perfectly balanced between Moses's self-delusion and the reality which he but imperfectly recognises. The last words are Moses's, and they bespeak Selvon's final codification of his hero: 'holding the cup up in the air I was still playing charades' (179).

Moses here is clearly more than a simple biblical archetype or a counter-racist symbol. He is a human being with all the attendant dreams, frailties, and vanities that we all have. Indeed, as the novel closes, Moses's life bespeaks a 'humanistic vision [which] extends beyond social concern, whether explicit or muted.'[19] For Selvon, Moses's odyssey is codified, not ended, as Moses recognises that the very 'charades' which have transformed him, have made him into a spokesman for the ceaseless universal complications of the human heart.

1 See Sam Selvon, *The Lonely Londoners* (Toronto: TSAR, 1991); *Moses Ascending* (Oxford: Heinemann, 1984); *Moses Migrating* (Harlow, Essex: Longman, 1983). Further references will be cited in the text.

2 Sam Selvon, in a guest lecture at the University of Calgary, January 1992, has said that initially he chose the name 'Moses' because it was typically Trinidadian in coming from the Bible, but in time he saw the appropriateness of the biblical archetype to his character.

3 See Clement H. Wyke, *Sam Selvon's Dialectal Style and Fictional Strategy* (Vancouver: University of British Columbia Press, 1991), and

Victor J. Ramraj, 'The Philosophy of Neutrality: The Treatment of Political Militancy in Samuel Selvon's *Moses Ascending* and *Moses Migrating*', in *Literature and Commitment: A Commonwealth Perspective*, ed. Govind Narain Sharma (Toronto: TSAR, 1988), pp.109-115. See also pp.77-84 of this book.

4 See Victor J. Ramraj, 'Selvon's Londoners: From the Centre to the Periphery', in *Language and Literature in Multicultural Contexts*, ed. by Satendra Nandan (Suva, Fiji: University of South Pacific, 1983), pp.297-306.

5 Edward W. Said, *The World, the Text and the Critic* (London: Faber & Faber, 1984), p.29.

6 Sam Selvon, 'Three into One Can't Go – East Indian, Trinidadian, and West Indian', in *Foreday Morning: Selected Prose 1946-1986*, Sam Selvon, ed. by Kenneth Ramchand and Susheila Nasta (Harlow, Essex: Longman, 1989), p.219.

7 Quoted in Kenneth Ramchand, 'Introduction', ibid., p.xi.

8 Ibid., p.xi.

9 'While all this confusion happening, Moses was killing himself with laugh [...].' Selvon, *The Lonely Londoners*, p.16.

10 'Now Moses is a veteran, who living in this country for a long time, and he meet all sorts of people and do all sorts of things, but he never thought the day would come when a fellar would land up from the sunny tropics on a powerful winter evening wearing a tropical suit and saying that he ain't have no luggage.' Ibid., pp.17f.

11 Addressing Henry, Moses says, 'I don't usually talk to fellars like this, but I take a fancy for you, my blood take you [...].' Ibid., p.21.

12 'Moses make up his mind to treat Galahad in a special way because he behaving as if he think he back home in Port of Spain or something. Still, he had to admit that it look as if Galahad have a lot of guts, the way how he getting on, the way how he land without any luggage, and Moses still amaze how he standing the cold without no winter clothes.' Ibid., p.19.

13 'Moses', he say, 'I too glad to see you, boy. If you don't mind I want you to come with me.'

'I thought so', Moses say. 'Boy, you lucky I have soft heart, else you never see me again as long as you stay in London. [...] Anyway, one thing is you must done with all this big talk.'

'Yes, yes,' Galahad say, so relieved to see Moses that he putting his hands on his shoulders like they is old pals.' Ibid., p.27.

14 'He don't know the right word, but he have the right feeling in his heart. As if the boys laughing, but they only laughing because they fraid to cry, they only laughing because to think so much about everything would be a big calamity – like how he here now, the thoughts so heavy like he unable to move his body.

Still, it had a greatness and a vastness in the way he was feeling tonight, like it was something solid after feeling everything else give way, and though he ain't getting no happiness out of the cogitations he still pondering, for is the first time that he ever find himself thinking like that.

[…] He watch a tugboat on the Thames, wondering if he could ever write a book like that, what everybody would buy.' Ibid., p.126.

15 Discovering Dominica leaving Jeannie's cabin, Moses knows that he spent the night while Bob has been seasick: he sees Dominica behaving the same as he has done with Jeannie, fearing Bob's discovery; Dominica gives his special laugh, and as Jeannie leaves the scene with blushes, Moses asks Dominica, 'How do you make that laugh of yours?' Selvon, *Moses Migrating*, p.49. The laugh allows Dominica to smooth over his upmanship with Moses even as Moses can use it to express his own surprise.

16 See ibid., pp.62f. and p.67.

17 See ibid., p.68.

18 See ibid., p.136.

19 Michel Fabre, 'Samuel Selvon', in *West Indian Literature*, ed. by Bruce King (London: Macmillan, 1979), p.5.

'OLDTALK': TWO INTERVIEWS WITH SAM SELVON

Almost every Sunday morning, like if they going to church, the boys liming in Moses room, coming together for an oldtalk, to find out the latest gen, what happening, when is the next fete...

The Lonely Londoners

1. SAMUEL SELVON INTERVIEWED BY JOHN THIEME

John THIEME: Sam Selvon, you did several other jobs before becoming a writer. Do you feel that these helped you very much in your career as a novelist?

Sam SELVON: Well, I think the experience during the war years, serving in the navy, did help me to collect myself and my thoughts. In terms of work after the war, I worked with the *Trinidad Guardian* as a journalist for five years and that did indeed help my writing. In fact it was during these years that I started writing short stories and poems.

THIEME: Were many of those published in the *Trinidad Guardian*?

SELVON: Quite a few were published. Some were broadcast by the BBC in London, in the *Caribbean Voices* programme.

THIEME: *Caribbean Voices* must have given a tremendous boost to your career in the fifties.

SELVON: It was the greatest thing that ever happened really, because the first thing that I ever sold for money was a poem that was broadcast by the BBC and I got a cheque for two guineas for it, which I swore that I would never spend.

THIEME: A lot of money in those days!

SELVON: In those days it was wonderful to have a cheque and to feel, well, I have written something that has been paid for.

THIEME: I know you remember Henry Swanzy very fondly. Do you have other mentors from that period?

SELVON: Yes, I remember even in those days Henry was a very great encouragement to me, because I got several stories broadcast by the BBC and when I decided to move to London, he wrote me a very encouraging letter, telling me he would do all he could to help me when I got there.

THIEME: Could you tell us a little about your early upbringing? One thinks of you sometimes in connection with V. S. Naipaul, because you're both at times comic writers and you both have a *kind of* East Indian background, but yours seems to have been very different from Naipaul's.

SELVON: Well, yes, I don't know. I think in a way my background is pretty nondescript. I'm working on an autobiographical novel. I have got sections of it finished. You see I grew up in Trinidad as a Trinidadian and my mother's father was a Scotsman and my father was an Indian. So I'm an offspring of that and I grew up in Trinidad completely westernised, completely creolised, not following any harsh, strict religious or racial idea at all.

THIEME: When you began to write, were you conscious of the need to write in an indigenous West Indian form? Were you from the outset trying to create something different from English fiction or did that come later?

SELVON: No, I don't think it was as deliberate as all that. What I was trying to do was to put Trinidad on the map. People didn't know what part of the world I came from and that was something that I felt ought to be corrected. Those days in England – in the fifties and so on – the only country in the Caribbean people spoke about was Jamaica. You never heard them talking about places like Barbados, Trinidad, Tobago and so on. So I felt it wasn't a question of going into the techniques of writing. It was just a story I wanted to tell, which was set in Trinidad in the first novel.

THIEME: It seems though that when you began to write about characters in an English setting, you did begin to go into the techniques and invent a new language form.

SELVON: Yes, I feel that the language is tied up so much with the characters that it is part of them, that just through language alone you can describe what type of people you're talking about. It's like having them speak. What I've been trying to do is convert this oral impression into a visual one, so that the page becomes a tape recorder as it were.

THIEME: I've often thought, that in addition to being generally rooted in oral storytelling, your fiction owes a particular debt to calypso, with its short episodic narratives.

SELVON: Yes, again that has not really been deliberate. My feeling is that it comes out that way, purely because of the society that I'm writing about. It's a Caribbean one and the people in Trinidad live calypso as part of their lives, their thoughts, their upbringing. And I suppose that this must necessarily come out in the writing. As you say, it's because these are the people I'm talking about and these are the people I'm writing about and this is the way the creation happens in my mind. They present themselves most truthfully in that form. So I use the form.

THIEME: You mentioned you're working on an autobiographical novel now. I've often wondered if there's an autobiographical element in the character of Tiger in those early novels.

SELVON: No. There was some feeling that maybe there was, but that wasn't really true, because I grew up in San Fernando from a middle-class background. But I know the cane villages and things like that so well that this is how I was able to write about it. Down south in Trinidad it's all sugar cane district – that's where I was born. Being so much in touch with what was happening around me. As I said, my upbringing was strictly creolised, but I learned how the Indians thought and it wasn't very difficult for me to imagine what it must have been like for Tiger to be forced into this marriage at an early age and to go through the whole ceremony. And of course the point of the story of Tiger isn't that he's an East Indian, but that he's a young man who is facing life and growing up and the things that happen to him could happen to any young boy, the thoughts that come to him: 'What should I do? I'm growing up to a man now? How should I face life? How should I face my responsibilities?' And things like that.

THIEME: Is there perhaps more of yourself in the character of Moses, who one feels at the end of *The Lonely Londoners* is a writer, as he stands back and looks at the world around him?

SELVON: Well, possibly – in the later books, *Moses Ascending* and *Moses Migrating*. I try to convey some of my own personal thoughts in my second

novel, *An Island Is a World*, which somehow isn't as popular as the others.
Most people seem to know my work through the first book, through Tiger
and through the character of Moses in the London novel, but I tried in
that second novel to put down some of my personal impressions about life
and there's still room for me to write such a novel. I want to write a novel
set in Trinidad that really describes the society very, very closely.

THIEME: Which of your novels that are currently out of print would you
most like to see reprinted? Would *An Island Is a World* be one?

SELVON: Yes, I would think *An Island Is a World*. Perhaps I shouldn't say
that because of the quality of the writing. It's a book I would like to rewrite very much. Of all the books I have written I would like to rewrite
that one, because I think that I never got to grips with what I was trying to
express in that book. But when you ask me which book reflects some of
my personal thoughts, I would say *An Island Is a World* and I would say *I
Hear Thunder*, both of which are set in middle-class society.

THIEME: You go back to Trinidad fairly frequently. How do you find the
Trinidad of today compares with the Trinidad you grew up in?

SELVON: It is changing. There is more hope I think. People in the young
generation are starting to think for themselves and ask questions. In that
respect I think there is a great deal of hope for the people in Trinidad.

THIEME: What prompted you to move to Calgary? Moses migrated back
to Trinidad, but you migrated to Calgary.

SELVON (Laughing):   Well, I lived in England for twenty-eight years,
which is almost half my lifetime. I had decided that it was time to get
back to the West. I wanted to get back into the Western hemisphere, not
necessarily the Caribbean, not necessarily Canada, not necessarily the
States. I didn't decide which country, but I wanted to get back into the
Western hemisphere, because I had lived so long in England and incul-
cated English literary values and tradition and custom and so on. I felt
that I was born in the West and I ought to get back into the Western way
of life. So I was going to leave England in four years from 1978, which
was the actual year that I left. But I had to leave in '78, because my wife
wanted to come to Canada right away. The reason I chose Canada – it's
just a domestic matter – is because she had relatives who were living
there before. So when we wanted to move she said 'Fine. Let's go over to
Canada.'

THIEME: Do you think you might ever write a novel about Canada?

SELVON: I certainly sincerely hope so. I would certainly be using Canada as a background to my future work.

THIEME: Have you discovered any affinities between the Canadian experience and the Caribbean, both being in the Western hemisphere?

SELVON: Yes. Very, very much so. Somehow in Canada I feel very, very close to the Caribbean, although strangely enough in terms of distance I am further away where I live now than when I lived in London. But there is something about the Western way of life, the Canadian way of life, which reminds me very much of the Caribbean. I find that the people from the Caribbean who live here in Canada are also different from those that live in London. They have a quicker acceptance here. They break down barriers much quicker.

THIEME: I'd like to ask you a little about the changes between *The Lonely Londoners* and *Moses Ascending*. One feels that the style of *Moses Ascending* is quite different from *The Lonely Londoners* in some way. Would you like to comment on what you were trying to do in *Moses Ascending*?

SELVON: What I was trying to do really was to try and push the language form that I used in *The Lonely Londoners* as far as I possibly could. When I was writing *The Lonely Londoners*, it wouldn't come at all in straight, Standard English. Eventually I decided to try to set the whole thing down, both the narrative and the dialogue, in this form of Caribbean language. And it just shot along. The book wrote itself in about six months, just like that. It was one of the fastest novels I've ever written. So in later years when I decided to do this sequel to *The Lonely Londoners*, it came back to me fine. The language worked so well with the first book, I decided I'm going to use it now, but I'm also going to show there's been some kind of development in Moses through all these years he's been living in England. I decided I'm going to use a kind of archaic English together with the dialogue format and see how the two would combine. And I think it has worked very well. The book was very well received and that kind of language use is what creates the book. I feel that you just cannot divorce people from the Caribbean from that language form, because it is so good that you see them instantly. So that it's like the page is talking to you.

THIEME: Have you finished with the character of Moses?

SELVON: I don't really know. I'm not sure. Although he is a successful character, I don't want to beat him to death. I have to think a little about this. I would like to turn my hand now to writing a novel in straight,

Standard English, possibly set in Trinidad, but with a wider range. I would also like part of it to happen here in Canada, perhaps in Toronto. So that the scene shifts from Toronto to Port of Spain – possibly include one or two of the other Caribbean islands – to give more of a bigger feeling of the Caribbean as a whole than just one island.

THIEME: What other West Indian writers do you particularly admire?

SELVON: Well, I think we have quite a few very good writers. I like Naipaul's work. I think he's one of the greatest writers alive. I like Lamming's work, particularly his earlier novels. And Andrew Salkey and some of the others. I'm not quite familiar with the work of all of them, because I don't do a very great deal of reading. I feel it might somehow impinge on my own personal thoughts and the things I want to write about. I don't like to read and find that something I want to write about has already been handled by another writer.

THIEME (Laughing):   You'd rather stay in ignorance?

SELVON: I'd rather stay in ignorance. Mark you, it may be true that I am repeating something that has been said before, but in the actual creation it wasn't so to me, because in my ignorance I didn't know. So I think that ignorance helps a lot. When you know that somebody has done something before, it hampers you.

THIEME: Perhaps we could conclude with a few questions on your 'English' books. One that I've always admired and feel has been neglected is *The Housing Lark*. It would seem to me to be a novel of the same calibre as *The Lonely Londoners*. Do you share that feeling?

SELVON: I like it. It followed swiftly on the heels of *The Lonely Londoners*. I think it's a very funny book and it also describes, perhaps in even greater detail than *The Lonely Londoners*, something of the hardships that the Caribbean people knew, particularly with housing and jobs and things like that. I'm hoping to get that reprinted. I'm hoping it will be reissued soon.

THIEME: *Ways of Sunlight* has, of course, remained a perennial favourite. The book is interesting because of the bipartite structure, with half in Trinidad and half in London...

SELVON: It has remained fairly popular. It's still in print.

THIEME: Do you see it as a unified volume or do you see it as a collection of pieces that just happened to come together?

SELVON: Well, it is unified in a way. Those London stories were written with the intention of eventually being put in a collection. The Trinidad ones are a bit more scattered, but they are not by any means all the short fiction I have written. I've got some others, which I scattered around in various anthologies and things like that.

THIEME: One last question: how did your perception of London change over the years you were there? It must have changed a great deal, if one takes *Moses Ascending* and *The Lonely Londoners* as any guide?

SELVON: Yes, it has changed over the years. I lived there for such a long time. When I first went to London, they were still issuing ration books and things like that. I love London. I got out of London what I had hoped for. Let me put it that way. Walking the streets of London and looking at the landscape...

THIEME: You were like Big City in *The Lonely Londoners*.

SELVON: Yes. What I wanted out of London, I got. I wasn't disappointed throughout all the years. I had difficult times sometimes – jobs and things like that – but by and large I love London. I've been back recently and it has changed a great deal from the London of the fifties. It's changed for the black immigrants and I think the actual landscape of the city has changed in certain parts.

THIEME: Sam, many thanks.

2. SAMUEL SELVON INTERVIEWED BY ALESSANDRA DOTTI

Alessandra Dotti: In *The Lonely Londoners* the characters try to adapt themselves to the city, they are looking for a solution to their problems. In *Moses Ascending* your vision of exile seems to have darkened. Moses himself is less positive and more isolated from his countrymen, struggling hard for total privacy. The ambivalent feeling towards London, the love/hate relationship with the town has grown into disillusion. In an interview with Professor John Thieme you said you loved London and that you got out of it what you had hoped for. Was your recourse to and the isolation in an intimate and inner world the main reason for your love of London and your success there?

Sam Selvon: Well, I always had a feeling for London from the time I was a child going to school, learning and reading about the English countryside and the English poets – Wordsworth and Keats and so on. I had a very great love for the English countryside although I had never known it at all, I had never seen it in my whole life; and one of the things that I did when I first went to London was to go out into the country districts, trying to see the flowers and the fields and the valleys and the landscapes that I read so much about. I found a great deal of satisfaction out of that... that love of London and the English countryside as a whole; I always felt a great feeling for it; I lived in London for twenty-eight years, which is a great part of my life spent there. As for the books, the difference between the two novels is a question of time really. *Moses Ascending* was written maybe twenty-five or thirty years after *The Lonely Londoners* and, in fact, when I did write *The Lonely Londoners* I had no idea in my mind that I would like to write a kind of sequel to it. In fact, I don't consider *Moses Ascending* to be a sequel. I just felt that I would use some of the same characters, that I would use Moses and Galahad and some of the others and update the situation of what was happening with the black communities in London. So really there is a big time gap between the time and the events of *The Lonely Londoners* to the later periods when I wrote *Moses Ascending*.

Dotti: However, in *Moses Ascending* your vision of exile seems to be more pessimistic and bitter.

Selvon: Did you say bitter? No, I don't think it shows, you know... particularly the hero, Moses... I was trying to create a character here who was ambivalent, who wasn't quite sure about life or about anything. He is a kind of universal figure. He is a figure of a man who doesn't quite know what he is going to do with his life, what is going to happen to him and things like that. In *Moses Ascending*, when he kind of withdraws, as you see, he does that, but at the same time he is necessarily involved in everything. I don't believe that any person in life… when you are living in a society or a community can withdraw yourself completely, how much you want to do that. Everyone in life reaches or has certain feelings at times when they want to be alone, they don't want to be with friends or anything, they have enough of that nonsense: listening to people's troubles, you know: 'My wife beat me last night; I had troubles with my wife last night', or, 'I had troubles at home'. This was the element that I wanted to bring out, that Moses just wanted to get off by himself a little. I also tried to show how difficult it is to do a thing like that, because he is involved, people want you to be involved. The ambivalence with Moses is that, in spite of his great desire for that, he inevitably becomes involved.

DOTTI: Is there anything of your experience as a writer in exile in the character of Moses in *Moses Ascending*?

SELVON: Well, there is a lot of… my own feelings reflected in a way the ambivalence of what life is all about. I don't like the word exile, I feel that when someone tells you that you are exiled that means that you are banished from your land. I just feel that I am living abroad, you know; I am living abroad as a writer. You see, the character of Moses was based entirely on a true figure, an alive, real figure, who was a Trinidadian that I met when I first came to London, and it's through him… he always wanted to write a book. He is the one who took me around, sort of put myself in shoes and things like that. Most of all I got was his experiences and a great deal of them are my mind too. I mean, I was one of the boys. A great deal of what happened to Moses also happened to me. All the experiences happened to me too while I lived in England. So I associate myself with that and with Moses to that extent.

DOTTI: But, is there anything of yourself as a writer in the character of Moses? I mean, in *Moses Ascending* Moses tries to write his memoirs and he is trapped between his desire to write about himself and his inner world and the need to write about his people and their struggle against racial prejudices.

SELVON: You have two characters here, you have Moses and the author myself. I wanted to write about the experiences of the black community.

Moses wanted to write something which is more personal, his whole life-story, which he never really wrote, as the book says. The book really says how he tries to write his memoirs but he never really got down to it; he was always involved with something else. I think that this is one of the aspects I wanted to bring out, that involvement with life, which is a universal thing that is very, very difficult. I don't think that Moses would have been the type of character who, even if he were completely isolated, would have been able to do very much writing. Sooner or later he would have felt: 'I wonder nobody is coming and see me,' and things like that. He lives in this kind of ambivalence, trapped between things.

DOTTI: Has this ambivalence of Moses influenced the structure of your novel? Moses himself, in fact, says: 'Naturally the whole structure of my work would have to be drastically altered if I was to incorporate these other aspects,' referring to the Black Power and the Blacks' struggles in Britain.

SELVON: This is quite true. Also another thing is… what I tried to do with that particular novel too is to extend the uses of language a great deal. I thought that, if Moses had lived so many years in England, he has taken in a great deal of English ways and mannerism and things like that, but only superficially because, you see, Moses is a very enigmatic character. A lot of people have still not quite understood all the ironies and the satire that is in the book. Some people are still wondering: 'Does Moses really love Britain?', or, 'Is he really an ambassador for Britain? That he always stands for Britain, at this point or another, but he doesn't…' As you know, in the later novel, *Moses Migrating*, where he sets himself as an ambassador for Britain and so, I mean, to me, me as the author, it's all a big joke, it's all a big ironic twist of the whole thing, because I think that Moses himself appreciates some of this irony too, but then he lives as if he were wearing a mask, a carnival mask. If you remember, in that particular novel, *Moses Migrating*, when his aunt tells him, at the end of the book: 'Moses you are always playing carnival, you are always wearing a mask. Nobody knows what you are really thinking inside yourself.'

DOTTI: I have greatly appreciated your short story 'My Girl and the City' where you deal with your creative process and communicate it to the reader. Was it hard work both to write about reality as it is, without 'weaving', and remain faithful to your original inspiration, that is, to 'what there was at the time'?

SELVON: With that particular short story, you know, I... this is more a
very personal aspect of my writing. When I first started to write, that is
how I wanted to write; I wanted to write in standard poetic English and
things like that. It is an aspect of my writing that I wanted to show for one
thing, and that I wanted to... I wouldn't say attempt, because I know that
I can write like that, but being involved and coming from Trinidad myself, wanting to write about the black communities and so on... this is
why I used that other kind of language for the novels, the Trinidad form
of English, because I felt that this was the best way to express their feelings and things like that. And in 'My Girl and the City', again in that particular story, as it shows, it comes back to your original question, my personal love, love of London too, you know... I love the city, I love things
about it. So really I myself as the author would be the counter to what I
am saying, would be a very ambivalent person too, in one way or the
other.

DOTTI: In 'My Girl and the City' as in your London novels, the traffic,
the underground, the buses, the people's faces are recurrent elements of
confusion and disturbance. As you say, 'motion mesmerises me into im-
mobility'. I got the impression that your characters are captured in a restless and swaying movement which always leaves and fixes them on the
same spot, strongly contributing to their feeling of loneliness and estrangement.

SELVON: That is true. Loneliness is a very personal thing and is a thing
that so many people suffer from. I was always aware, for instance, in my
living in London, how isolated I was with my thoughts and my feelings.
Millions of people moving to and fro, day by day, doing their things and
so on, and, if you consider each of them, they are all locked away, just like
a mass movement of people, but there is no cohesion about it. When you
get out of the tube station, as I did in 'My Girl and the City', once you get
out of the underground of London and then you reach the street, then
everyone separates, they go off to their different lives. So you get this impression in the facts of life; vast numbers of black people who have settled
in England, that they suffer this kind of loneliness.

DOTTI: In *The Lonely Londoners* as in *Moses Ascending* there is a general
want of love. Is it due to the hardships the characters must face – the lack
of a house, of a permanent job – or to a generalised inner incapacity of a
deep sentimental involvement?

SELVON: Well, I don't think so. When you say love you mean something that is deep and intimate perhaps, but the way the Caribbean people live, you know, they express… they are general that way. It is not a thing that they become very personal about, but there is, for instance, a great love between Moses and Galahad; he likes Galahad, this is why he does these things for him.

DOTTI: Yes, but I mean, there is a general want of love between men and women. Your 'boys' never enter into a lasting relationship with the girls they meet.

SELVON: Yeah, I quite agree with you. I mean, I wasn't going to write a love story. There were no characters that fell in love with their white girls. I think their relationship, that relationship between the black men and the English girls, the white girls, that was only superficial, that was satisfactorily sexual, there was no… I don't think that… Moses never met a girl that he became emotionally drawn to; none of the characters, not even Bart, when he says he must find that girl again, the girl that he was… there is still that difference between them, there isn't that sort of emotional love thing that you would get perhaps in a love story, which would be something else.

DOTTI: In your novels there are very few fully-realised female characters, while your male characters' search for identity usually merges with the simple desire to assert their masculinity. Women are seen only as sexual objects. Is there any relationship with the calypso tradition in which the male is a sort of phallic symbol?

SELVON: Not really. Many people had said that I hadn't written very much about women in the book, but, I mean, that would be another novel – I could write a novel like that. But while I was writing this book, I mean, this is the way that things really happened, this is the way that things were. If I wanted, as a writer, if I planned to write a novel to show also the woman's point of view, how the woman was making out in London herself and so on, the black woman, I would have written a different kind of novel, but that wasn't the concept I had of the novel. I didn't want to write something that one would say is a fully-drawn novel, which depicts each and every aspect of the black community life living in a white society. I wrote it just as it happened during this time, in a natural way. This is really how it was. That is not to say that there isn't a lot of… that things were not happening with black women here and so, but, as I said, this would have been another kind of story.

DOTTI: The deep humanity of your characters has often escaped the notice of the critics. Is it due to the comic way in which you deal with them and which seems to wrap and entangle them within the limits of realism?

SELVON: I don't think that the humorous side of the novels has very much to do with that. That is part of the characteristics of West Indian people, you know; they like to make fun, they like to try and look at the light side of life, to offset the hardships and tribulations that they undergo. A comment like that means that you are seeing it from an aspect of your culture and what you would consider to be humanity really, and things like that, but that kind of commentary has never been made by people from the Caribbean, because they understand and they see it. You were looking at it from the point of view of your culture.

DOTTI: But I found a great and deep humanity in your characters in spite of, or, perhaps, because of the comic way in which you deal with them. However, the critics have too often considered them as mere caricatures.

SELVON: Well, I think so. What can I tell you? You know, those things are there and they are implied. It is good to me that you had been able to see that, because there is a great deal of it. When you consider that, in spite of the humour and the hardships and everything... that these people still have some affection for one another, they would do things for one another, the basic things, that people from a Third World country, who had been implanted into a white society, that they still hold together to some extent, that they still try to keep some value and some worth and humanity. It is good that you were able to see it, because I think all of that I tried to suggest in the novels.

DOTTI: It seems to me that there is also a great sadness underneath the humour and the comedy. Is that true?

SELVON: Well, that too could be. It's really a universal sadness. When you move out of your country into another one, into a strange one, into a different kind of society, into a different world completely, you know, that is so different from what you are accustomed to. There must be naturally loneliness. There would be sadness, a feeling of... a kind of estrangement away from reality, and this is a thing that you have to learn to live with. When you move out of one culture into another, you experience all these things; and it isn't only that black people experience it in a white society. I think that anyone, white or black, who moves out of his culture into another has these difficulties as well.

DOTTI: Professor John Thieme said that though it does not include any episodes from an actual carnival, *The Lonely Londoners* may reasonably be viewed as the seminal West Indian carnival text either for the language or the characters' lifestyle. But carnival, which represents a healthy subversion to the British value system, becomes a means of self-evasion in a country which lacks any form of carnivalesque suspension. Is it a challenge to the system or a proud return to Trinidadian tradition?

SELVON: I think so. The carnival is a national part of the culture of Trinidad and that all exuberance and everything, that you say… it is something that in a steady English society they are not accustomed to… the ways and mannerisms of these people who live a different kind of life; and there is a contrast. I agree with what has been said there.

DOTTI: In your novels there is no linear development; they do not proceed towards a traditional conclusion. Do you intentionally react to the usual structure of the European novel or do you rather perceive how reality does not offer positive resolutions?

SELVON: Well, let me too answer this one quite honestly. Well, you know, what is a novel? I never conceived of the book to take the shape of a novel. In fact most of the novels that I have started just stem out of a general idea that develops as it goes along. In that particular novel, *The Lonely Londoners*, the way I wanted to write it is just as it was written; I never had any feeling at the back of my mind that it was going to take the traditional form or style of what is conceived as the novel. I wrote it as it came to me. I just put it down just like that, and it could be said to be a series of episodes and anecdotes that I tried to bring all together, which haven't one character or a main character. But it certainly… it was accepted as a kind of novel in that sense, it hadn't anything to do with what I would say the traditional forms, but the way the story evolved, this is how it was, this is how it happened in my mind; I just put it down like that.

DOTTI: If you were to write another novel would you still make use of that witty and humorous mixture of Standard English and creolised Trinidadian dialect?

SELVON: I think so. I think that if I write about people from the Caribbean in my novels in the future… to me language is very, very important, and this is the way that they speak, and this is the way that they think…

that I would have from time to time to use that form of language form in my work. In fact, even if you look at *The Lonely Londoners* there are sections of it which are written, or start off at least, in standard poetic English, and then I work my way into getting into the minds and the psyches of these people through the language that they use; and therefore it becomes very important to me that in any future work that I am doing, if I have Caribbean characters and I feel it is necessary to use their language form, I will certainly use it. So I think that I would certainly say yes, I would use that form whenever I think it is necessary. Let me just add that sometimes it's very difficult; for instance, I feel to lead up into something I would need to use Standard English, to lead up to a situation or something like that, but once I get into the minds of the characters, if they are Caribbean people, I think to the language change; then immediately it identifies them, and you think aloud with them; and I think it enhances the whole thing.

DOTTI: Would you ever write about people other than the Caribbean ones and so use a standard form of English?

SELVON: Of course, it would be necessary, if I don't only want to write the books about Caribbean people. But, you see, I am a Caribbean man myself and it is the psyche that I know best, so that other characters from other cultures would really be superficial to some extent. I don't think that, even if I have lived abroad for so many years, I could really get into the psyche of – say – an English person, an English man, to write with that depth of feeling that I can bring out in my Caribbean characters, to bring out a depth or anything out of the English psyche, because I don't know it. It isn't my culture and in that sense I would always try to stay with what I know best. This is why, wherever I go, I think I would be writing in a universal way to have my characters be universal too, but I think that the language... There are times when I feel that it is necessary for me to use that language form.

DOTTI: Do you think that the relationship between blacks and whites has improved in England since the 1950s and 1970s?

SELVON: I would have thought so up to the time that I left in the late 1970s; there were signs that it was being recognised more, but I... having left the country and so, you know, things have happened that I don't know anything about... so I don't know. But from reports that I hear now I think that – and this is very saddening to me – that... I don't think that things have improved very much, because there are still a great deal of blatant black/white prejudices existing in the country.

DOTTI: Are things better in Canada?

SELVON: I would say so. I think Canada is a fairly new country and although there is prejudice… You see, Canada is a different country entirely. England is really an island, as an island it is divided. In Canada you have a vast continent that is divided into provinces; it is almost like the Caribbean where you have islands and you move from an island to another, and you move from one province to another… It's a different kind of country. It's a country of immigrants. It's a country made up of people who moved from other parts of the world and came to settle in Canada. So that the immigrant from the Caribbean who goes to Canada feels as if, well, he is also another immigrant into the country. I think that on the whole the Canadians tend to look upon one another in that way. So that there is really not that sort of blatant prejudice you would get as in England where the English would feel: 'Here all these black people are invading us… in the country.'

DOTTI: Do you find the contribution of Caribbean literature more easily accepted in Canada than in England?

SELVON: I think it has been accepted all over the world, all over the English speaking world.

DOTTI: Yes, but I mean, as a contribution to English and world literature, not as a second-class literature.

SELVON: No, I think it is English literature. After all it is written in English – or in forms of English. I feel that Caribbean literature as such… perhaps we have started to build a tradition of literature that comes out of our part of the world, out of the West Indies and the Caribbean – the English speaking part of it – but it contributes a great deal to world literature. I think that there is on the whole a tendency for the bigger countries to learn and understand more. I think that literature is doing a very great job in helping people to understand what is happening in other parts of the world. Well, here we are, here you are interviewing me and I am from a small island, Trinidad, that nobody would have known anything about unless the writers had started to come out and write something about it.

DOTTI: Do you think that the concept of Third World literature, with all its implications, is deeply rooted in England?

SELVON: I myself, I don't like the term Third World really, you know. We have got one world to live in and they make three. I feel that say – writing from my region of the world… it comes from a part that hasn't been… that few people have known very much about. And now people know more. I think the world is getting to be a smaller place in that sense, populations are exchanging cultures, they are exchanging literatures, they are learning more about each other and also the feeling of universality, which is what most writers try for. I think also that Caribbean writers in their way are struggling for this, in a way, that they want to be aligned with universality; they don't want to be left apart as a separate kind of culture. I think we all have something to contribute.

DOTTI: In an interview with Peter Nazareth you said that in America the writing is much fresher; more dynamic and creative than in England.

SELVON: Well, I don't know. I think that, well… dynamism in the sense that it is more profitable to be writing in America. I think that in both sides, that in America too there is a great increase in order to find out more about these other countries, and about the literatures and the writers that come from these other countries. So I think on the whole that, as well as literature goes in the last twenty years or so, great strains have been made towards accomplishing this; I mean, European and other writers, they are making researches in literatures, or are visiting the Caribbean more, or are visiting other parts of the world, finding out about the cultures and these people and things like that. So I think, as I say, in that sense the writers and the literature have done a great deal to make that commendable.

DOTTI: Well, Mr. Selvon, many thanks.

BIBLIOGRAPHY

1. Primary Sources

With regard to the primary sources listed below I am heavily indebted to Susheila Nasta whose pioneering and most thorough bibliography I was kindly permitted to reprint from *Foreday Morning: Selected Prose 1946-1986*, edited by Kenneth Ramchand and Susheila Nasta (Harlow, Essex: Longman, 1989).

1.1. Novels

A Brighter Sun (London: Allan Wingate, 1952; New York: Viking Press, 1953; London: Longman, 1971; Harlow, Essex: Longman, 1985).

An Island Is a World (London: Allan Wingate, 1955; Harlow, Essex: Longman, 1983; Toronto: TSAR, 1993; London: TSAR, 1994).

The Lonely Londoners (London: Allan Wingate, 1956; New York: St. Martin's Press, 1957. Reprinted under the title *The Lonely Ones*, London: Brown and Watson, 1959, and again as *The Lonely Londoners*, London: Mayflower Books, 1967; London: Longman, 1972; Harlow, Essex: Longman, 1985; Toronto: TSAR, 1991).

Turn Again Tiger (London: MacGibbon and Kee, 1958; New York: St. Martin's Press, 1959; London: Four Square, 1962; London: Heinemann, 1979).

I Hear Thunder (London: MacGibbon and Kee, 1963; New York: St. Martin's Press, 1963).

The Housing Lark (London: MacGibbon and Kee, 1965; Washington, D.C.: Three Continents Press, 1987).

The Plains of Caroni (London: MacGibbon and Kee, 1970; Toronto: Williams Wallace, 1985).

Those Who Eat the Cascadura (London: Davis-Poynter, 1972; Toronto: TSAR, 1990).

Moses Ascending (London: Davis-Poynter, 1975; London: Heinemann, 1984).

Moses Migrating (London: Longman, 1983; Harlow, Essex: Longman, 1987; Washington, D.C.: Three Continents Press, 1992).

1.2. SHORT STORIES

In the entries below reference is made to the first appearance of the story and to
any reprinting in some of the various anthologies of Caribbean writing. Up to
date there are two collections of Sam Selvon's short stories: *Ways of Sunlight* (Lon-
don MacGibbon and Kee, 1957; London: Longman, 1973; Harlow, Essex,
Longman, 1985. The references below are made to the 1973 edition), and *Foreday
Morning: Selected Prose 1946-1986*, ed. by Kenneth Ramchand and Susheila Nasta
(Harlow, Essex: Longman, 1989). Many of the short stories listed below were
also broadcast by the BBC *Caribbean Voices* programme produced by Henry
Swanzy (1948-1956). The recordings and script numbers are held by the BBC
Script Library, Caversham, Reading, England.

'The Christmas Gift', *Guardian Weekly* (Trinidad), 22 December 1946.
   Reprinted in *Foreday Morning*, 58-61.
'Echo in the Hills', *Trinidad Guardian*, 26 January 1947.
   Reprinted in *Foreday Morning*, 62-65.
'Rhapsody in Red', *Trinidad Guardian*, 9 and 16 March 1947.
   Reprinted in *Foreday Morning*, 66-76.
'Steelband' (by Ack-Ack alias Sam Selvon), *Guardian Weekly* (Trinidad), 24 May
   1947.
'For Love of Mabel', *Evening News*, 14 June 1947.
   Reprinted in *Guardian Weekly* (Trinidad), 6 July 1947.
'And Then There Were None', also called 'The Sea' (by Ack-Ack alias Sam
   Selvon), *Guardian Weekly* (Trinidad), 21 September 1947.
   Reprinted in *Foreday Morning*, 77-82.
'Boomerang' (by Big Buffer alias Sam Selvon), *Guardian Weekly* (Trinidad), 19
   October 1947.
   Reprinted in *Foreday Morning*, 83-86.
'Carnival Last Lap' (by Ack-Ack alias Sam Selvon), *Trinidad Guardian*, 8 Febru-
   ary 1948.
'The Great Draught', BBC *Caribbean Voices*, 29 February 1948.
   Early and different version as 'A Drink of Water' in *Ways of Sunlight*, 112-
   121.
   Reprinted in *Foreday Morning*, 87-90.
'Obeah Man' (by Ack-Ack alias Sam Selvon), *Trinidad Guardian*, 29 February
   1948.
   Reprinted in *Foreday Morning*, 91-95.
'Pandee Pays a Visit', *Guardian Weekly* (Trinidad), 21 March 1948.

'Murder Will Out' (by Ack-Ack alias Sam Selvon), *Guardian Weekly* (Trinidad), 25 April 1948.

    Also published as 'Dry River Murder' in 1949.

    Reprinted in *Foreday Morning*, 96-99.

'Passing Cloud' (by Denmar Cosel alias Sam Selvon), *Guardian Weekly* (Trinidad), 19 September 1948.

    Reprinted in *Foreday Morning*, 100-103.

'Johnson and the Cascadura', *Guardian Weekly* (Trinidad), 11 October 1948.

    Expanded version including love interest in *Ways of Sunlight*, 11-37.

    Reprinted in *Foreday Morning*, 104-111.

'Julia's Happy Christmas', *Evening News*, 21 December 1948.

'The Baby', *Bim*, 3:10 (1949), 106-109.

'Dry River Murder', same as 'Murder Will Out' (1948), *West Indian Review*, 1:16 (1949), 16-17.

'What's the Use', *Bim*, 3:11 (1949), 182-184.

    Reprinted in *Foreday Morning*, 112-115.

'Cane is Bitter', *Bim*, 4:13 (1950), 56-59.

    Incorporated in *A Brighter Sun*.

    Reprinted in:

    Ways of Sunlight, 59-73.

    Caribbean Anthology of Short Stories, ed. by [anon] (Kingston: The Pioneer Press, 1953), 56-58.

    London Magazine, 5:1 (1958), 14-24.

    Stories from the Caribbean, ed. by Andrew Salkey (London: Paul Elek, 1965); this collection was published under the title *Island Voices: Stories from the West Indies* (New York: Liveright, 1970), 59-70.

    From the Green Antilles: Writings of the Caribbean, ed. by Barbara Howes (London: Souvenir Press, 1967), 125-137.

    Best West Indian Stories, ed. by Kenneth Ramchand (London: Nelson Caribbean, 1982), 117-127.

'Roy, Roy', *Guardian Weekly* (Trinidad), 9 April 1950.

'Finding Picadilly Circus', *Guardian Weekly* (Trinidad), 17 December 1950.

    Early immigrant story absorbed in *The Lonely Londoners*.

    Reprinted in *Foreday Morning*, 123-126.

'Harper's Happy Christmas', *Guardian Weekly* (Trinidad), 23 December 1951.

    Reprinted in *Foreday Morning*, 116-119.

'Poem in London', BBC *Caribbean Voices*, 1951.

    Reprinted in *Foreday Morning*, 127-133.

'Talk', *Bim*, 4:15 (1951), 151-153.

    Incorporated in *An Island is a World*.

'Day of the School', BBC *Caribbean Voices*, 3 February 1952.

    Reprinted in *Foreday Morning*, 134-138.

'Five Rivers', *Guardian Weekly* (Trinidad), 17 February 1952.

    Shorter Version of 'Holiday in Five Rivers', published in *Ways of Sunlight*, 50-58.

    Reprinted in *Foreday Morning*, 139-141.

'Calypsonian', *Bim*, 5:17 (1952), 40-47.

    Reprinted in:

    Foreday Morning, 142-154.

    West Indian Stories, ed. by Andrew Salkey (London: Faber and Faber, 1960), 106-117.

    Caribbean Literature: An Anthology, ed. by G. R. Coulthard (London: University of London Press, 1966), 72-83.

    Caribbean Rhythms: The Emerging English Literature of the West Indies, ed. by James T. Livingston (New York: Washington Square Press, 1974), 86-98.

    Literary Glimpses of the Commonwealth, ed. by James B. Bell (Toronto: Wiley Publishers, 1977), 173-188.

    London Magazine, under the title 'Song of Sixpence', 7:8 (1960), 35-44.

    Tiger's Triumph: Celebrating Sam Selvon, ed. by Susheila Nasta and Anna Rutherford (Hebden Bridge: Dangaroo Press, 1995), 24-32.

    The Penguin Book of Caribbean Short Stories, ed. by E. A. Markham, under the title 'Song of Sixpence' (London: Penguin, 1996), 134-145.

    Published with London setting as 'Calypso in London', in *Ways of Sunlight*, 125-131.

'The Mouth-Organ', BBC *Caribbean Voices*, 27 December 1952.

    Reprinted in *Foreday Morning*, 155-159.

'A Child's Christmas', BBC *Caribbean Voices*, 27 December 1953.

'Knock and Enter', *Guardian Weekly* (Trinidad), 29 March 1953.

    Ends like 'Gussy and the Boss'.

'Foster and the Coronation', BBC *Caribbean Voices*, 31 May 1953.

'The Little Men', *Bim*, 6:21 (1954), 56-58.

    Reprinted in *Foreday Morning*, 160-165.

'The Mango Tree', BBC *Caribbean Voices*, 27 February 1955.

'Behind the Humming Bird', *Bim*, 6:23 (1955), 165-171.

    Version of 'Wartime Activities', published in *Ways of Sunlight*, 82-93.

'Come Back to Grenada', BBC *Caribbean Voices*, 27 December 1955.

    Material worked into *The Lonely Londoners*.

    Reprinted in:

    Foreday Morning, 166-177.

London Magazine, 3:9 (1956), 25-32.

Tamarack Review, 14 (1960), 15-26.

'Gussy and the Boss', *Bim*, 6:22 (1955), 68-71.

   Reprinted in:

   Ways of Sunlight, 104-111.

   Stories from the Caribbean, ed. by Andrew Salkey (London: Paul Elek, 1965); this collection was later published under the title *Island Voices: Stories from the West Indies* (New York: Liveright, 1970), 53-59.

   West Indian Stories, ed. by John Wickham (London: Ward Lock Educational, 1981), 58-66.

'Voodoo in Grove', *Evening Standard*, 12 June 1957.

   Similar to 'Obeah in the Grove' in *Ways of Sunlight*, 167-174.

'The Boy Who Made the Rains Come', *Evening Standard*, 26 July 1957.

   Reprinted in *Foreday Morning*, 178-181.

'My Girl and the City', *Bim*, 7:25 (1957), 2-6.

   Reprinted in:

   Ways of Sunlight, 181-188.

   West Indian Stories, ed. by Andrew Salkey (London: Faber and Faber, 1960), 98-105.

   From the Green Antilles: Writings of the Caribbean, ed. by Barbara Howes (London: Souvenir Press, 1967), 138-144.

   Best West Indian Stories, ed. by Kenneth Ramchand (London: Nelson Caribbean, 1982), 180-185.

   Tiger's Triumph: Celebrating Sam Selvon, ed. by Susheila Nasta and Anna Rutherford (Hebden Bridge: Dangaroo Press, 1995), 96-101.

   The Penguin Book of Caribbean Short Stories, ed. by E. A. Markham (London: Penguin, 1996), 146-152.

Ways of Sunlight (London MacGibbon and Kee, 1957; London: Longman, 1973; Harlow, Essex, Longman, 1985).

   Contains:

   'Johnson and the Cascadura', 11-37.

   'Down the Main', 38-49.

   'Holiday in Five Rivers', 50-58.

   'Cane is Bitter', 59-73.

   'The Village Washer', 74-81.

      Reprinted in *The Sun's Eye: West Indian Writing For Young Readers*, comp. by Anne Walmsley (London: Longman, 1968), 52-59; New Edition (London: Longman, 1989), 45-51.

   'Wartime Activities', 82-93.

   'The Mango Tree', 94-103.

'Gussy and the Boss', 104-111.

'A Drink of Water', 112-121.

> Reprinted in *Caribbean Stories: Fifteen Short Stories by Writers from the Caribbean*, ed. by Michael Marland (London: Longman, 1978), 98-105.

'Calypso in London', 125-131.

> Reprinted in *New Statesman*, 53 (5 January 1957), 10-11.

'Working the Transport', 132-138.

'Waiting for Auntie to Cough', 139-145.

> Reprinted in:
>
> *West Indian Stories*, ed. by Andrew Salkey (London: Faber and Faber, 1960), 118-124.
>
> *The Routledge Reader for Caribbean Literature*, ed. by Alison Donnell and Sarah Lawson Welsh (London: Routledge, 1996), 231-236.

'Eraser's Dilemma', 146-150.

> Reprinted in *Literature of the World*, ed. by Thelma G. James et al. (New York: McGraw Hill, 1963), 347-350.

'Brackley and the Bed', 151-155.

> Reprinted in:
>
> *West Indian Narrative: An Introductory Anthology*, ed. by Kenneth Ramchand (London: Nelson, 1966), 100-105.
>
> *Carray*, ed. by James Lee Wah (London: Macmillan, 1977), 104-108.

'If Winter Comes', 156-160.

'The Cricket Match', 161-166.

> Reprinted in *The Oxford Book of Caribbean Short Stories*, ed. by Stewart Brown and John Wickham (Oxford and New York: Oxford University Press, 1999), 91-95.

'Obeah in the Grove', 167-174.

> Reprinted in:
>
> *The Minority Experience*, ed. by Michael Marland (London: Longman, 1978), 114-121.
>
> *This Island Place*, ed. by Robert Fraser (London: Harrap, 1981), 76-82.

'Basement Lullaby', 175-180.

> Reprinted in *New Statesman*, 54 (17 August 1957), 196-198.

'My Girl and the City', 181-188.

'Knock on Wood', *Evergreen Review*, 3:9 (1959), 25-34.

> Reprinted in *West Indian Stories*, ed. by Andrew Salkey (London: Faber and Faber, 1960), 68-97.

'The Cultivated Carib', *Bim*, 7:28 (1959), 224-230.

'Whip Round', *Reveille*, 18 February 1965.

'Man in England, You've Just Got to Love Animals', in *Stories from the Caribbean*,
    ed. by Andrew Salkey (London: Paul Elek, 1965); this collection was later
    published under the title *Island Voices: Stories from the West Indies* (New York:
    Liveright, 1970), 45-50.

'When Greek Meets Greek', in *Stories from the Caribbean*, ed. by Andrew Salkey
    (London: Paul Elek, 1965); this collection was later published under the ti-
    tle *Island Voices: Stories from the West Indies* (New York: Liveright, 1970), 50-
    53.

'Her Achilles Heel', *Words*, 10 (1980), 51-54.

    Reprinted in:
    Foreday Morning, 182-189.
    Ambit, 91 (1982), 4-8.

'Ralphie at the Races', *Ariel*, 13:4 (1982), 117-128.

    Reprinted in *Foreday Morning*, 190-201.

'Going Back Home', *World Literature Written in English*, 21:2 (1982), 392-405.

'The Harvester', *Toronto South Asian Review*, 5:1 (1986), 21-31.

'Zeppi's Machine', *A Shapely Fire: Changing the Literary Landscape*, ed. by Cyril
    Dabydeen (Oakville, Ontario: Mosaic Press, 1987), 19-31.

1.3. Unfinished Novels and Manuscripts

'Turning Christian' [unfinished novel started in 1986], in *Foreday Morning: Se-
    lected Prose 1946-1986*, ed. by Kenneth Ramchand and Susheila Nasta
    (Harlow, Essex: Longman, 1989), 202-210.

[Extract from an Unfinished Novel], *Ariel*, 27:2 (April 1996), 11-20.

[Extract from an Unfinished Autobiography], *Ariel*, 27:2 (April 1996), 20-23.

1.4. Children's Books

Carnival in Trinidad (Wellington: Department of Education, 1964).

A Cruise in the Caribbean (Wellington: Department of Education, 1966).

A Drink of Water (London: Nelson, 1968).

    Originally published in *Ways of Sunlight*, 112-121.

1.5. Poems

Some of the poems listed below were also broadcast by the BBC *Caribbean Voices* programme produced by Henry Swanzy (1948-1956). The recordings and script numbers are held by the BBC Script Library, Caversham, Reading, England.

'The Empty Glass', *Trinidad Review*, 15 December 1946.
'Petranella', *Trinidad Review*, 12 January 1947.
'I Vow Madness', *Trinidad Guardian*, 26 January 1947.
'Success', *Trinidad Guardian*, 2 February 1947.
'Fear', *Trinidad Guardian*, 9 February 1947.
'Come Back', *Trinidad Guardian*, 16 February 1947.
'Poui Tree', *Trinidad Guardian*, 2 March 1947.
'Words and Hearts', *Trinidad Guardian*, 23 March 1947.
'Consolation', *Trinidad Guardian*, 13 April 1947.
'Wings of Thought', *Trinidad Guardian*, 20 April 1947.
'Dream', *Trinidad Guardian*, 11 May 1947.
'Landscape', *Trinidad Guardian*, 25 May 1947.
'Gravediggers', *Trinidad Review*, 25 May 1947.
'Life With You', *Trinidad Guardian*, 20 July 1947.
'At Tacarigua', *Trinidad Guardian*, 24 August 1947.
'Rain', *Trinidad Guardian*, 14 September 1947.
'Sun', *Bim*, 3:2 (1949), 249.
    Reprinted in:
    Tamarack Review (1960), 5.
    Tiger's Triumph: Celebrating Sam Selvon, ed. by Susheila Nasta and Anna
        Rutherford (Hebden Bridge: Dangaroo Press, 1995), 54.
'Variation', *Bim*, 5:20 (1954), 299.
    Reprinted in *Breaklight: Caribbean Poetry* (London: Hamish Hamilton,
        1971), 145.
'Discovering the Tropic', in *Caribbean Voices: An Anthology of West Indian Poetry*,
    ed. by John Figueroa (London: Evans Brothers, 1971), 160-164.
'For Frank Collymore', *Savacou*, 7/8 (1973), 25.

1.6. Non-fiction and Talks

Some of the non-fictional texts listed below are included in *Foreday Morning: Selected Prose 1946-1986*, ed. by Kenneth Ramchand and Susheila Nasta (Harlow, Essex: Longman, 1989). All radio talk scripts are held by BBC Script Library, London.

'We Join the Navy', *Guardian Weekly* (Trinidad), 14 December 1946.
    Extracts reprinted in *Foreday Morning*, 3-5.
'The Last Outpost', *Guardian Weekly* (Trinidad), 10 January 1947.
    Reprinted in *Foreday Morning*, 6-9.
'The House We Lived In' (by Michael Wentworth alias Sam Selvon), *Evening News*, 23 January 1947.
    Reprinted in *Foreday Morning*, 15-18.
'As Time Goes By' (by Michael Wentworth alias Sam Selvon), *Evening News*, 20 March 1947.
    Reprinted in:
    Foreday Morning, 23-26.
    Bim, 3:12 (1950), 322-324.
    Caribbean Prose: An Anthology for Secondary Schools, ed. by Andrew Salkey (London: Evans Brothers, 1967), 22-27.
'A Man I Remember' (by Michael Wentworth alias Sam Selvon), *Evening News*, 27 March 1947.
    Reprinted in *Foreday Morning*, 10-14.
'The Life of a Day', *Evening News*, 10 May 1947.
    Reprinted in *Foreday Morning*, 33-37.
'The Story of a Tree', *Evening News*, 7 June 1947.
    Reprinted in *Foreday Morning*, 27-29.
'Ralph Will Try Again', *Evening News*, 9 July 1947.
    Reprinted in *Foreday Morning*, 54-57.
'Some Trinidad Birds', *Evening News*, 31 August 1947.
    Extracts reprinted in *Foreday Morning*, 30-32.
'Michael Wentworth Contends', *Evening News*, 18 November 1947.
    Reprinted in *Foreday Morning*, 50-53.
'Holidays at Aunt Polly' (by Michael Wentworth alias Sam Selvon), *Evening News*, 10 December 1947.
    Reprinted in *Foreday Morning*, 19-22.
'The Same Old Life', *Evening News*, 18 January 1948.
    Reprinted in *Foreday Morning*, 43-46.

'He Is Going to Die', (by Michael Wentworth alias Sam Selvon), *Evening News*, 21 February 1948.

Reprinted in *Foreday Morning*, 38-42.

'These People Are Fatalists' (by Esses alias Sam Selvon), *Port of Spain Gazette*, 13 March 1948.

Reprinted in *Foreday Morning*, 47-49.

'The Leaf in the Wind', *Bim*, 4:16 (1952), 286-287.

Reprinted in:

Critical Perspectives on Sam Selvon, ed. by Susheila Nasta (Washington, D.C.: Three Continents Press, 1988), 55-56.

Tiger's Triumph: Celebrating Sam Selvon, ed. by Susheila Nasta and Anna Rutherford (Hebden Bridge: Dangaroo Press, 1995), 62.

'Village in the Bambbees', *Tea-Time Talk*, BBC Radio Broadcast, 19 June 1952.

'English Goes Abroad – English as Spoken in the West Indies', *The English Tongue*, BBC Radio Broadcast, 30 August 1955.

'British Caribbean Writers', Samuel Selvon in Discussion with Stuart Hall, BBC Radio Broadcast, 21 April 1958.

'North Atlantic – Volcanoes and Coral Islands', *Exploration Earth* (script by Selvon), BBC Radio Broadcast, 12 December 1966.

'Little Drops of Water', *Bim*, 11:44 (1967), 245-252.

Reprinted in:

Caribbean Essays: An Anthology, ed. by Andrew Salkey (London: Evans Brothers, 1973), 100-107.

Critical Perspectives on Sam Selvon, ed. by Susheila Nasta (Washington, D.C.: Three Continents Press, 1988), 57-62.

'Samuel Selvon Discusses *Those Who Eat the Cascadura* with Ronald Bryden', British Institute of Recorded Sound, Tape No. M 1770 W.

'A Note on Dialect', in *Commonwealth*, ed. by Anna Rutherford (Aarhus: Aarhus University Press, 1971), 124.

Reprinted in:

Critical Perspectives on Sam Selvon, ed. by Susheila Nasta (Washington, D.C.: Three Continents Press, 1988), 63.

Tiger's Triumph: Celebrating Sam Selvon, ed. by Susheila Nasta and Anna Rutherford (Hebden Bridge: Dangaroo Press, 1995), 74.

'Sam Selvon Talks to Gerald Moore', *The English Novel Abroad* (Interview and Reading), BBC Radio Broadcast, 1 January 1974.

'Sam Selvon Talks to Norman Jeffares', *Commonwealth Writers*, (London: British Council Literature Department, Tape No. 1993, recorded 1975).

'Sam Selvon Reads and Talks about his Work', recording made at Annual Conference of the Association for the Teaching of Caribbean and African

Literature, 24 September 1982 (London: British Institute of Recorded Sound).

'Three Into One Can't Go: East Indian, Trinidadian or West Indian', *Wasafiri*, 5 (1986), 8-12.

Reprinted in:

India in the Caribbean, ed. by David Dabydeen and Brinsley Samaroo (London: Hansib, 1987), 13-24.

Foreday Morning, 211-225.

'Finding West Indian Identity in London', *Kunapipi*, 9:3 (1987), 34-39.

Reprinted in *Tiger's Triumph: Celebrating Sam Selvon*, ed. by Susheila Nasta and Anna Rutherford (Hebden Bridge: Dangaroo Press, 1995), 58-61.

1.7. PLAYS AND FILMS

The entries below are listed according to the year of broadcast. All radio play scripts are held by the BBC Radio Library London.

Basement Lullaby (1958), adptn. for radio by Peggy Walls of the story in *Ways of Sunlight*, 175-180.

Screenplay for *The Lonely Londoners*; commissioned by Robert Parish Enterprises, 1958.

Lost Property (1965), adptn. for radio by Sam Selvon of 'Eraser's Dilemma', published in *Ways of Sunlight*, 146-150.

Perchance to Dream (1966), adptn. for radio by Sam Selvon of 'Brackley and the Bed', published in *Ways of Sunlight*, 151-155.

Rain Stop Play (1967), adptn. for radio by Sam Selvon of 'The Cricket Match', published in *Ways of Sunlight*, 161-166.

Highway in the Sun (1967), adptn. for radio by Sam Selvon of *A Brighter Sun*.

You Right in the Smoke (1968), original script for radio.

Eldorado West One (1969), 7 part adptn. for radio by Sam Selvon of *The Lonely Londoners*.

The World of Sam Selvon (1969), scripted by the author for Trinidad Theatre Workshop.

Bringing in the Sheaves (1969), original script for radio.

Home Sweet India (1970), adptn. for radio by Sam Selvon of *An Island Is a World*. Also adapted for television play, BBC 2, London 1976.

Turn Again Tiger (1970), adptn. for radio by Sam Selvon of the novel *Turn Again Tiger*.

Voyage to Trinidad (1971), original script for radio.

Those Who Eat the Cascadura (1971), adptn. for radio by Sam Selvon of 'Johnson and the Cascadura', published in *Ways of Sunlight*, 11-37.

The novel of the same title as the radio play was published in 1972.

Mary, Mary Shut Your Gate (1971), original script for radio.

Cry Baby Brackley (1972), original script for radio.

Water for Veronica (1972), adptn. for radio by Sam Selvon of 'A Drink of Water', published in *Ways of Sunlight*, 112-124.

The Harvest in the Wilderness (1972), adptn. for radio by Sam Selvon of *The Plains of Caroni*.

Anansi, The Spider Man (1974), television play for BBC 1, London 1974.

Milk in the Coffee (1975), original script for radio.

Zeppi's Machine (1977), original script for radio.

Switch (1977), stage play performed at the Royal Court Theatre, London.

Co-author with Horace Ové (director), of script for the film *Pressure*, (London: British Film Institute, on general release in 1978).

Eldorado West One, ed. and introd. by Susheila Nasta (Leeds: Peepal Tree Press, 1988).

Highway in the Sun and Other Plays (Leeds: Peepal Tree Press, 1991).

Contains:

'Highway in the Sun', 4-52.

'Turn Again Tiger', 53-95.

'Home Sweet India', 97-130.

'The Harvest in Wilderness', 131-183.

2. Secondary Sources

There are some entries below which deserve preliminary mentioning. Both *Critical Perspectives on Sam Selvon* (ed. by Susheila Nasta) and *Tiger's Triumph: Celebrating Sam Selvon* (ed. by Susheila Nasta and Anna Rutherford) include a number of seminal essays and interviews. The same is true for the April 1996 edition (27:2) of *Ariel*, which in addition to critical works also includes tributes to Sam Selvon. Apart from a very few PhD theses there are only three book-length studies on Selvon's oeuvre: Mark Looker's *Atlantic Passages: History, Community, and Language in the Fiction of Sam Selvon*, Clement H. Wyke's *Sam Selvon's Dialectal Style and Fictional Strategy*, and Roydon Salick's groundbreaking interpretations in *The Novels of Samuel Selvon: A Critical Study*.

2.1. Critical Works

Barratt, Harold, 'An Island Is Not a World: A Reading of Sam Selvon's *An Island Is a World*', *Ariel*, 27:2 (April 1996), 25-34.
— 'Sam Selvon's Tiger: In Search of Self-Awareness', in *Reworlding: The Literature of the Indian Diaspora*, ed. by Emmanuel S. Nelson (New York: Greenwood Press, 1993), 105-114.
— 'From Colony to Colony: Selvon's Expatriate West Indians', in *Critical Perspectives on Sam Selvon*, ed. by Susheila Nasta (Washington, D.C.: Three Continents Press, 1992), 250-259.
— 'Dialect, Maturity, and the Land in Sam Selvon's *A Brighter Sun*: A Reply', in *Critical Perspectives on Sam Selvon*, ed. by Susheila Nasta (Washington, D.C.: Three Continents Press, 1992), 187-195.
— 'West Indian and South African: The Committed Individual in Selvon, Lovelace, Anthony and Coetzee', in *Literature & Commitment: A Commonwealth Perspective*, ed. by Govind Narain Sharma (Toronto: TSAR, 1988), 26-33.
— 'Individual Integrity in Selvon's *Turn Again Tiger* and *Those Who Eat the Cascadura*', *Toronto South Asian Review*, 5:1 (1986), 153-160.
Baugh, Edward, 'Friday in Crusoe's City: The Questions of Language in Two West Indian Novels of Exile', in *Critical Perspectives on Sam Selvon*, ed. by Susheila Nasta (Washington, D.C.: Three Continents Press, 1992), 240-249.
— 'Belittling the Great Tradition, in Good Humour', in *The Comic Vision in West Indian Literature*, ed. by Roydon Salick (San Fernando: Printex, 1988), 1-9.

— 'Exiles, Guerrillas and Visions of Eden', *Queen's Quarterly*, 84 (Summer 1977), 273-286.

Bernhardt, Stephen A., 'Dialect and Style Shifting in the Fiction of Samuel Selvon', in *Studies in Caribbean Language*, ed. by Lawrence D. Carrington et al. (St. Augustine, Trinidad: Society for Caribbean Linguistics, 1983), 266-276.

Birbalsingh, Frank, 'Samuel Selvon and the West Indian Literary Renaissance', *Ariel*, 8:3 (1977), 5-22.

Brathwaite, E. K., 'Sir Galahad and the Islands', in *Critical Perspectives on Sam Selvon*, ed. by Susheila Nasta (Washington, D.C.: Three Continents Press, 1992), 19-28.

Brown, Wayne, '"A Greatness and a Vastness": The Search for God in the Fiction of Sam Selvon', *Ariel*, 27:2 (April 1996), 35-46.

Chang, Victor, 'Elements of the Mock-Heroic in West Indian Fiction: Samuel Selvon's *Moses Ascending* and Earl Lovelace's *The Dragon Can't Dance*', in *Re-siting Queen's English: Essays Presented by John Pengwerne Matthews*, ed. by Gillian Whitlock and Helen Tiffin (Amsterdam: Rodopi, 1992), 91-101.

Chen, Willi, 'A Night with Sam Selvon', *London Magazine*, 34:5-6 (1994), 99-103.

Chukwu, Augustine Emmanuel, 'Home and Exile: A Study of the Fiction of Sam Selvon' (unpublished doctorial dissertation, The University of New Brunswick, 1984; abstract in *Dissertation Abstracts International*, 45 (June 1985), 3651A).

Clarke, Austin, *A Passage Back Home: A Personal Reminiscence of Samuel Selvon* (Toronto: Exile Editions, 1994).

Clarke, Austin, Jan Carew, Ramabai Espinet, Ismith Khan and Frank Birbalsingh, 'Sam Selvon: A Celebration', *Ariel*, 27:2 (April 1996), 49-63.

Davies, Barrie, 'The Sense of Abroad: Aspects of the West Indian Novel in England', *World Literature Written in English*, 2:2 (1972), 67-81.

Dotti, Alessandra, 'Illusione e identitá nella narrativa di Samuel Selvon' (unpublished doctorial thesis, University of Milan, 1988).

Dickinson, Swift Stiles, 'Sam Selvon's "Harlequin Costume": *Moses Ascending*, Masquerade, and the Bacchanal of Self-Creolization', *MELUS: The Journal of the Society for the Study of the Multi-Ethnic Literature of the United States*, 21:3 (Fall 1996), 69-106.

— 'Transnational Carnival and Creolized Garden: Caribbean Cultural Identity and Rooting in the Narratives of Sam Selvon and Merle Hodge' (unpublished doctorial dissertation, Washington State University, 1994; abstract in *Dissertation Abstracts International*, 56 (December 1995), 2246a).

Ellis, David, 'The Produce of More Than one Country: Race, Identity, and Discourse in Post-Windrush Britain', *Journal of Narrative Theory*, 31:2 (Summer 2001), 214-232.

— 'Writing Home: Black Writing in Britain Since the War' (unpublished doctorial dissertation, University of Essex, 1993; abstract in *Dissertation Abstracts International*, 55 (Winter 1994), 1046).

Esty, Joshua Dwight, 'The Shrinking Island: English Modernism and the Culture of Imperial Decline' (unpublished doctorial dissertation, Duke University, 1996; abstract in *Dissertation Abstracts International*, 57 (June 1997), 5163).

Fabre, Michel, 'From Trinidad to London: Tone and Language in Samuel Selvon's Novels', in *Critical Perspectives on Sam Selvon*, ed. by Susheila Nasta (Washington, D.C.: Three Continents Press, 1992), 213-222.

— 'Moses and the Queen's English: Dialect and Narrative Voice in Samuel Selvon's London Novels', *World Literature Written in English*, 21:2 (Summer 1982), 385-392.

— 'Samuel Selvon', in *West Indian Literature*, ed. by Bruce King (London: Macmillan, 1979), 152-162.

— 'The Queen's Calypso: Linguistic and Narrative Strategies in the Fiction of Samuel Selvon', *Commonwealth: Essays and Studies*, 3 (1977-78), 69-76.

Gikandi, Simon, 'Beyond the *Kala-pani*: The Trinidad Novels of Samuel Selvon', in *Writing in Limbo: Modernism and Caribbean Literature* (Ithaca and London: Cornell University Press, 1992), 107-138.

Gonzalez, Anson, 'First of the Big Timers: Samuel Selvon', in *Critical Perspectives on Sam Selvon*, ed. by Susheila Nasta (Washington, D.C.: Three Continents Press, 1992), 44-51.

Gowda, H. H. Anniah, 'A Brief Note on the Dialect Novels of Sam Selvon and Earl Lovelace', *Literary Half-Yearly*, 27:2 (July 1986), 98-103.

Grant, Jane W., *Sam Selvon: Ways of Sunlight* (London: Longman, 1979).

Hall, Stuart, 'Lamming, Selvon, and Some Trends in the West Indian Novel, *Bim*, 6:23 (1955), 172-178.

Ingrams, Elizabeth, '*The Lonely Londoners*: Sam Selvon and the Literary Heritage', *Wasafiri*, 33 (Spring 2001), 33-36.

James, Louis, 'Writing the Ballad: The Short Fiction of Samuel Selvon and Earl Lovelace', in *Telling Stories: Postcolonial Short Fiction in English*, ed. by Jacqueline Bardolph (Amsterdam: Rodopi, 2001), 103-108.

Jones-Petithomme, Moya, 'Forty Years Hence: Immigrants and Yardies in Selvon and Headley', *Matatu: Journal for African Culture and Society*, 12 (1994), 35-44.

Joseph, Margaret Paul, *Caliban in Exile: The Outsider in Caribbean Fiction* (New York: Greenwood, 1992).

— 'Caliban's Double Exile' (unpublished doctorial dissertation, Temple University, 1990; abstract in *Dissertation Abstracts International*, 51 (May 1991), 3738).

Khan, Ismith, 'Remembering Sammy', in *Tiger's Triumph: Celebrating Sam Selvon*, ed. by Susheila Nasta and Anna Rutherford (Hebden Bridge: Dangaroo Press, 1995), 1-23.

Kuhlmann, Deborah J., 'Selvon's "Come Back to Grenada": Bridges and Boundaries', *Griot: Official Journal of the Southern Conference on Afro-American Studies*, 17:2 (Fall 1998), 38-42.

Looker, Mark, *Atlantic Passages: History, Community, and Language in the Fiction of Sam Selvon* (New York: Peter Lang, 1996).

Loreto, Paola, 'The Male Mind and the Female Heart: Selvon's Ways to Knowledge in the "Tiger Books"', *Caribana*, 5 (1996), 117-125.

— 'Sam Selvon', *Caribana*, 4 (1994-1995), 115-116.

Macdonald, Bruce F., 'Language and Consciousness in Samuel Selvon's *A Brighter Sun*', in *Critical Perspectives on Sam Selvon*, ed. by Susheila Nasta (Washington, D.C.: Three Continents Press, 1992), 173-186.

Mair, Christian, 'Contrasting Attitudes Towards the Use of Creole in Fiction – a Comparison of Two Early Novels by V. S. Naipaul and Sam Selvon', in *Crisis and Creativity in the New Literatures in English*, ed. by Geoffrey Davis and Hena Maes-Jelinek (Amsterdam: Rodopi, 1990), 133-149.

Martin, John Stephen, 'The Odyssey of Sam Selvon's Moses', in *Nationalism vs. Internationalism: (Inter)National Dimensions of Literatures in English*, ed. by Wolfgang Zach and Ken L. Goodwin (Tübingen: Stauffenburg, 1996), 399-405.

McGoogan, Ken, 'Saying Goodbye to Sam Selvon', *Ariel*, 27:2 (April 1996), 65-75.

Morris, Mervyn, 'Introduction', in *Moses Ascending*, by Sam Selvon (Oxford, Heinemann, 1975), vii-xviii.

Mühleisen, Susanne, 'How to Translate Creole: Choices in German Translations of Anglo-Creolophone Texts', in *Making Meaningful Choices in English: On Dimensions, Perspectives, Methodology and Evidence*, ed. by Rainer Schulze (Tübingen: Gunter Narr, 1998), 139-156.

Naipaul, V. S., 'Caribbean Voices – *An Island Is a World*', in *Critical Perspectives on Sam Selvon,* ed. by Susheila Nasta (Washington, D.C.: Three Continents Press, 1992), 112.

Nasta, Susheila and Anna Rutherford (eds), *Tiger's Triumph: Celebrating Sam Selvon* (Hebden Bridge: Dangaroo Press, 1995).

Nasta, Susheila, 'Crossing Over and Shifting the Shapes: Sam Selvon's Londoners', in *Home Truths: Fictions of the South Asian Diaspora in Britain* (Basingstoke, Hampshire: Palgrave, 2002), 56-92.

— 'Setting Up Home in a City of Words: Sam Selvon's London Novels', in *Tiger's Triumph: Celebrating Sam Selvon*, ed. by Susheila Nasta and Anna Rutherford (Hebden Bridge: Dangaroo Press, 1995), 78-95.

— 'Samuel Selvon: Prolific! Popular!', in *Moses Migrating*, by Sam Selvon (Washington, D.C.: Three Continents Press, 1992), 181-201.

— (ed.), *Critical Perspectives on Sam Selvon* (Washington, D.C.: Three Continents Press, 1992).

— '*The Lonely Londoners*', in *A Handbook for Teaching Caribbean Literature*, ed. by David Dabydeen (London: Heinemann, 1987), 23-34.

Nazareth, Peter, 'The Clown in the Slave Ship', in *Critical Perspectives on Sam Selvon*, ed. by Susheila Nasta (Washington, D.C.: Three Continents Press, 1992), 234-239.

Okereke, Grace Eche, 'Samuel Selvon's Evolution From *A Brighter Sun* to *Turn Again Tiger*: An Expansion of Vision and a Development of Form', in *Tiger's Triumph: Celebrating Sam Selvon*, ed. by Susheila Nasta and Anna Rutherford (Hebden Bridge: Dangaroo Press, 1995), 35-50.

Page, Malcolm, 'West Indian Writers', *Novel: A Forum on Fiction*, 3:2 (1970), 167-172.

Phillips, Caryl, 'Following On: The Legacy of Lamming and Selvon', *Wasafiri*, 29 (Spring 1999), 34-36.

Pouchet Paquet, Sandra, 'An Introduction to *Turn Again Tiger*', in *Critical Perspectives on Sam Selvon*, ed. by Susheila Nasta (Washington, D.C.: Three Continents Press, 1992), 196-212.

— 'Samuel Dickson Selvon', in *Fifty Caribbean Writers: A Bio-bibliographical Critical Sourcebook*, ed. by Daryl Cumber Dance (New York: Greenwood Press, 1986), 439-450.

Poynting, Jeremy, 'Samuel Selvon, *Moses Migrating*', in *Critical Perspectives on Sam Selvon*, ed. by Susheila Nasta (Washington, D.C.: Three Continents Press, 1992), 260-265.

— 'A Comedy of Impersonation', *World Literature Written in English*, 23:2 (1984), 424-429.

Ramchand, Kenneth, 'The Love Songs of Samuel Dickson Selvon', *Ariel*, 27:2 (April 1996), 77-88.

— 'Introduction', in *An Island is a World*, by Sam Selvon (Toronto: TSAR, 1993), v-xxv.

— 'Song of Innocence, Song of Experience: Samuel Selvon's *The Lonely Londoners* as a Literary Work', in *Critical Perspectives on Sam Selvon*, ed. by Susheila Nasta (Washington, D.C.: Three Continents Press, 1992), 223-233.

— 'Introduction', in *Foreday Morning: Selected Prose 1946-1986*, by Sam Selvon (Harlow, Essex: Longman, 1989), viii-xviii.

— 'Comedy as Evasion in the Later Novels of Sam Selvon', in *The Comic Vision in West Indian Literature*, ed. by Roydon Salick (San Fernando: Printex, 1988), 31-48.

— 'An Introduction', in *The Lonely Londoners*, by Sam Selvon (Harlow, Essex: Longman, 1985), 3-21.

— 'The Fate of Writing in the West Indies: Reflections on Oral and Written Literature', *Caribbean Review*, 11:4 (1982), 16-17, 40-41.

— 'A Brighter Sun', in *An Introduction to the Study of West Indian Literature* (London: Nelson, 1976), 58-72.

— *The West Indian Novel and Its Background* (London: Faber and Faber, 1970).

Ramraj, Victor, 'The Philosophy of Neutrality: The Treatment of Political Militancy in Samuel Selvon's *Moses Ascending* and *Moses Migrating*', in *Literature and Commitment: A Commonwealth Perspective*, ed. by Govind Narain Sharma (Toronto: TSAR, 1988), 109-115.

— 'Selvon's Londoners: From the Centre to the Periphery', in *Language and Literature in Multicultural Contexts*, ed. by Satendra Nandan (Suva, Fidji: University of South Pacific, 1983), 297-306.

Rohlehr, Gordon, 'Samuel Selvon and the Language of the People', in *Critics on Caribbean Literature*, ed. by Edward Baugh (London: George Allen & Unwin, 1978), 153-161.

— 'The Folk in Caribbean Literature', in *Critical Perspectives on Sam Selvon*, ed. by Susheila Nasta (Washington, D.C.: Three Continents Press, 1988), 29-43.

Salick, Roydon, *The Novels of Samuel Selvon: A Critical Study* (Westport, Connecticut: Greenwood Press, 2001).

— 'Sam Selvon's *I Hear Thunder*: An Assessment', *Ariel*, 27:2 (April 1996), 117-129.

— 'Selvon and the Limits of Heroism: A Reading of *The Plains of Caroni*', in *Tiger's Triumph: Celebrating Sam Selvon*, ed. by Susheila Nasta and Anna Rutherford (Hebden Bridge: Dangaroo Press, 1995), 102-113.

— 'Selvon's Santiago: An Intertextual Reading of *The Plains of Caroni*', *Journal of West Indian Literature*, 5:1-2 (August 1992), 97-105.

— 'Introduction', in *A Brighter Sun*, by Sam Selvon (Harlow, Essex: Longman, 1985).

Singh, Vishnudat, 'The Returning Immigrant and Tourist: Or Selvon and the Semiotics of Tourism', in *The Comic Vision in West Indian Literature*, ed. by Roydon Salick (San Fernando: Printex, 1988), 10-18.

Srivastava, Aruna, 'Images of Women in Indo-Caribbean Literature', in *Indenture & Exile: The Indo-Caribbean Experience*, ed. by Frank Birbalsingh (Toronto: TSAR, 1989), 108-114.

Sutherland, R., 'Sam Selvon – The Caribbean Connection', *Toronto South Asian Review*, 2:1 (1983), 44-46.

Tabuteau, Eric, *Images du multiculturisme dans le romans antillais anglophone: Wilson Harris, George Lamming, V. S. Naipaul, Sam Selvon* (Villeneuve d'Ascq: Presses Universitaires du Septentrion, 1999).

— 'Love in Black and White: A Comparative Study of Samuel Selvon and Frantz Fanon', *Commonwealth: Essays and Studies*, 16:2 (Spring 1993), 88-95.

Thieme, John, '"The World Turn Upside Down": Carnival Patterns in *The Lonely Londoners*', *The Toronto South Asian Review*, 5 (Summer 1986), 191-204.

Thorpe, Michael, 'Sam Selvon (1923-1994)', *World Literature Today*, 69:1 (Winter 1995), 86-88.

Tiffin, Helen, '"Under the Kiff-Kiff Laughter": Stereotype and Subversion in *Moses Ascending* and *Moses Migrating*', in *Tiger's Triumph: Celebrating Sam Selvon*, ed. by Susheila Nasta and Anna Rutherford (Hebden Bridge: Dangaroo Press, 1995), 130-139.

— 'Post-Colonial Literatures and Counter-Discourse', *Kunapipi*, 9:3 (1987), 17-33.

Van Sertima, Ivan, 'Samuel Selvon', *Caribbean Writers: Critical Essays* (London: New Beacon Books, 1968), 42-44.

Warner-Lewis, Maureen, 'Samuel Selvon's Linguistic Extravaganza: *Moses Ascending*', in *Critical Issues in West Indian Literature*, ed. by Erika Sollish Smilowitz and Roberta Quarles Knowles (Parkersburg, IA: Caribbean Books, 1984), 101-111.

Watling, Gabrielle, 'Embarrassing Origins: Colonial Mimetism and the Metropolis in V. S. Naipaul's *The Mimic Men* and Sam Selvon's *Moses Ascending*', *LINQ*, 20:2 (1993), 68-77.

Wiggan, Katherine, 'Comedy and Creole in Selvon's London Stories', in *The Comic Vision in West Indian Literature*, ed. by Roydon Salick (San Fernando: Printex, 1988), 19-25.

Wyke, Clement H., 'Voice and Identity in Sam Selvon's Late Short Fiction', *Ariel*, 27:2 (April 1996), 133-148.

— *Sam Selvon's Dialectal Style and Fictional Strategy* (Vancouver: University of British Columbia Press, 1991).

2.2. INTERVIEWS

Birbalsingh, Frank, 'Samuel Selvon: The Open Society or Its Enemies?', in *Frontiers of Caribbean Literatures in English*, ed. by Frank Birbalsingh (New York: St. Martin's, 1996), 54-67.

Dasenbrock, Reed and Feroza Jussawalla, 'Interview with Sam Selvon', in *Tiger's Triumph: Celebrating Sam Selvon*, ed. by Susheila Nasta and Anna Rutherford (Hebden Bridge: Dangaroo Press, 1995), 114-125.

Durix, Jean-Pierre, 'Talking of *Moses Ascending* with Samuel Selvon', *Commonwealth: Essays and Studies*, 10:2 (Spring 1988), 11-13.

Fabre, Michel, 'Samuel Selvon: Interviews and Conversations', in *Critical Perspectives on Sam Selvon*, ed. by Susheila Nasta (Washington, D.C.: Three Continents Press, 1988), 64-76.

Nasta, Susheila, 'The Moses Trilogy: Sam Selvon Discusses His London Novels', *Wasafiri*, 1:2 (1986), 5-10.

Nazareth, Peter, 'Interview with Sam Selvon', in *Critical Perspectives on Sam Selvon*, ed. by Susheila Nasta (Washington, D.C.: Three Continents Press, 1988), 77-94.

Ramchand, Kenneth, 'Sam Selvon Talking: A Conversation with Kenneth Ramchand', in *Critical Perspectives on Sam Selvon*, ed. by Susheila Nasta (Washington, D.C.: Three Continents Press, 1988), 95-103.

— 'Interview with Sam Selvon', *The Express* (Trinidad), 13 June 1982, 16-17.

Roberts, Kevin and Andra Thakur, 'Christened with Snow: A Conversation with Sam Selvon', *Ariel*, 27:2 (April 1996), 89-115.

Stone, Rosemary, 'Interview with Samuel Selvon', *The Express* (Trinidad), 2 March 1972, 13.

Thieme, John and Alessandra Dotti, '"Oldtalk": Two Interviews with Sam Selvon', *Caribana*, 1 (1990), 71-84.

Ursulet, J., 'An Interview with Sam Selvon', *Afram Newsletter*, 13 (1981), 14-16.

Wyke, Clement H., 'Interview with Samuel Selvon', *Chimo*, (Spring 1981), 30-38.

LIST OF CONTRIBUTORS

HAROLD BARRATT, former Professor of English and Chairman of Languages and Letters at the University College of Cape Breton, Nova Scotia, Canada.

ALESSANDRA DOTTI, graduate from the University of Milan, Italy, with a dissertation on Sam Selvon.

PAOLA LORETO, Assistant Professor of American Literature at the University of Milan, Italy.

JOHN STEPHEN MARTIN, Professor Emeritus at the University of Calgary, Canada.

SUSHEILA NASTA, Research Lecturer at the Open University in Milton Keynes, England.

KENNETH RAMCHAND, Professor at the Department of English at the University of the West Indies, St. Augustine, Trinidad.

VICTOR J. RAMRAJ, Professor at the Department of English at the University of Calgary, Canada.

JOHN THIEME, Professor of English Studies at South Bank University, London.

MAUREEN WARNER-LEWIS, Professor of African-Caribbean Language and Orature in the Department of Literatures in English at the University of the West Indies, Mona, Jamaica.

MARTIN ZEHNDER, MA graduate in Colonial and Postcolonial Literature from the University of Warwick, England.

INDEX